And the Angels Danced:

The Sermons and Writings of Lance Ness

Rev. Lance Ness

Parson's Porch Books

www.parsonsporchbooks.com

And the Angels Danced

ISBN: Softcover 978-1-951472-08-5

Copyright © 2019 by Lance Ness

All rights reserved. No part of this book may be reproduced or transmitted in any form or by any means, electronic or mechanical, including photocopying, recording, or by any information storage and retrieval system, without permission in writing from the publisher.

And the Angels Danced

Contents

Sermons Matter 7

Articles

Hell-Free Evangelism 9
"Noah" Knows Nothing 12
A Study in "Out of the Saltshaker and into the World" 15
A Precious Gift 17
One Last Word About Christmas 19
Independence Day 2010 21

Poems

And the Angels Danced 24
Iron Teeth 26
A Life in Christ 27
Techno Terror 29

Sermons

Is There A God? 31
Who Was Jesus and Why Did He Die on a Cross? 48
What is God Really Like? 55
Do I Have to Go to Church? 64
Each One A Minister 73
Advent Season: Add A Vent 73
Christmas Eve: Light In The Darkness 85
Good Friday: The Ultimate Transfusion 89
Easter Sunday: The Empty Tomb 93
Worldwide Communion Sunday: The History of Bread 100

Yom Kippur: The Two Goats 106
The Greatest Commandment: Love 112
God Always Does the Wrong Thing 119
Temptation 124
Watch Your Mouth 131

Funeral Resources

My Personal Funeral Experiences 138

Short Stories

The Legend of the Snowsnake 151
Those Who Were Not Wise 156

Sermons Matter

Parson's Porch Books is delighted to present to you this series called Sermons Matter.

We believe that many of the best writers are pastors who take the role of preacher seriously. Week in, and week out, they exegete scripture, research material, write and deliver sermons in the context of the life of their particular congregation in their given community.

We further believe that sermons are extensions of Holy Scripture which need to be published beyond the manuscripts which are written for delivery each Sunday. Books serve as a vehicle for the sermon to continue to proclaim the Good News of the Morning to a broader audience.

Lance Ness provides us great examples of what diligent study and weekly preparation provide to the crafting of excellent sermons.

We celebrate the wonderful occasion of the preaching event in Christian worship when the Pastor speaks, the People listen and the Work of the Church proceeds.

Take, Read, and Heed.

David Russell Tullock, M.Div., D.Min.
Publisher
Parson's Porch Books

Hell-Free Evangelism

Recently I went to a seminar to learn more about evangelism; the Christian practice of telling people the "good news" of Jesus Christ and trying to convert them to Christianity. I watched a video in which a Christian would talk with people on the street and ask them questions. Part of this video shows the Christian talking a great deal about heaven and hell.

I don't wish to scorn this particular form of evangelism because I know it does work, but I do have some trouble with it. I often feel it portrays God in a rather negative manner and it doesn't work all the time. In fact, during the video, one young man stated that he was not a believer and he did not want to become a believer out of fear. I can very much identify with that man because I was in the exact same position at one time.

Discussing our faith publicly is not the only form of evangelism but it is very effective. But as I watched the video I wondered if there wasn't a method to publicly witness to people that does not involve fear or guilt.

I believe there is. As I watched this video I began to think about my own father. My father died when I was two years old. The only memories I have of him are the testimony of relatives and friends telling me what my father was like. Apparently, he was a very good man and a great father. Growing up without him was a very difficult thing. I do find comfort in believing that, one day, I will enter heaven, meet my father, and spend eternity with him and with many other friends and relatives who have gone on before me.

However, that comforting fact has never made my life easier. I am quite certain my childhood and teen years would have been much better if I had my father's influence in my life. If someone could give me the option of living my life over again and give me the option of living my life with or without my father, I think my choice would be quite obvious. Call me greedy but if I could I would choose a <u>life</u> with my father, followed by an <u>eternity</u> with my father.

That's why I sometimes find it so hard to believe the choices people make in their lives today. So many people seem to feel they can live their lives in whatever way they choose and then spend eternity with God. There are many people out there who will certainly argue with that kind of belief. But even if that belief is true, my question to you is, "why are you choosing to only meet God after you're dead?" Why not meet God now, while you're alive, so you can have a lifetime with God <u>AND</u> then have an eternity with God?

Christianity is not just about where you go after you die. Jesus came to show us how to have a life with God <u>today</u>. I had to learn the hard way that life can be difficult and trying to live life "your way" often leads to trouble. But living life God's way, living a life in which God is central to your life, makes life far more rewarding, far more comforting, and it sees you through the hard times.

Do you sometimes feel like you're already living in hell? Maybe you are. According to Jewish teachings hell is not exactly a place. Hell is about being far from God's love. By ignoring God you are cheating yourself out of a far more enjoyable, far more rewarding, life. To borrow a phrase from another minister, you are settling for "fast food" when you could be having a "real meal" with God every day.

You are also cheating God. God wants to be in our lives. When we turn our backs on God, we deprive God of what God wants.

Why wait until you die? You can know God's love and presence today. You can trade in hell for a little bit of heaven right now.

Yes, following God means giving some things up and taking on a new way of life. That can be scary for some people but what do you have to lose? Trade in waiting for an eternity with God to live a life with God today <u>AND</u> spend eternity with God. Trade in a petty, empty, or self-centered life for a life with God. Find a life that is rewarding, exciting, and far more worthwhile.

In Jesus' Name

"Noah" Knows Nothing

I saw the movie "Noah" (2014) with my friend Jim the other day. As we left the theater he jokingly commented, "Well, his name was Noah. Other than that..." His comment was quite accurate. Although you can say the movie was inspired by the Biblical story, most of the movie is as far from the Bible as the east is from the west. (It's almost like saying the character Sponge Bob Square Pants is inspired by the fact that there are living sponges in the sea. Other than that...) "Noah" doesn't "Know A" lot about the Bible.

The movie begins by telling that God created the universe, then Adam and Eve, and they had 3 sons; Cain, Abel and Seth. Cain murdered Abel and was punished by God. These events are genuinely recorded in the Bible. From there the movie goes on to say how all the descendents of Cain were wicked and Noah was chosen because he was the last descendent of Seth. The Bible says all people had become wicked and Noah was chosen because he was righteous, not because of his ancestry.

The movie then moves into a pro-environment theme and I started to roll my eyes; this is definitely not from the Bible. The most glaring example of a departure from the Bible involves strange rock monsters called "Watchers" who helped Noah build the Ark and protected him from the descendents of Cain. This is absolutely not from the Bible.

But in many ways the most disturbing aspect of the movie is found in Noah's belief that he was called only to save the animals and after the flood Noah and his family would be the last of humanity, destined to die out and leave the earth as it was "meant to be." This is flagrantly contrary to the Bible. In fact I might argue it's a wicked teaching.

Overall, I enjoyed the movie as an adventure movie, but I knew many people who have never read the Bible would watch this and think it's an accurate telling of the Bible story.

I was right. Some people believe this is what the Bible says because they saw it in a movie. In fact many people are accepting some movies that are inspired by history as factual when they are not. The movie "JFK" is an ideal example. It does contain many historically accurate statements and facts so it may seem to be a very accurate rendering of events surrounding the Kennedy assassination. In reality it is so full of fallacy and speculation that it cannot be taken seriously. It is not history.

We should not be getting our "facts" from movies. We should be studying and seeking the truth.

You might need to spend hours to do a decent study of the JFK assassination, but the entire Noah story takes up just a few pages in the Bible; Genesis chapters 6-9. The whole story can be read in minutes.

Please show this article to friends and neighbors who saw the "Noah" movie, especially if they do not attend a church. Many people already have many false beliefs and understandings about the Bible; we don't want people developing more. It is especially important that the people who call themselves Christians be ready to stand up and speak the truth; tell the real stories and show the world what Christianity truly means. The Noah story may seem to tell the tale of a cruel God wiping out millions of lives, but there is another way to look at the story.

God saw the great wickedness in the human heart and real history supports this. Untold atrocities have happened because of the evil in the human heart. But we have a God who chose to spare humanity rather than wipe us all out. There have been many moments when all humanity could have been wiped out by diseases or natural disasters. This is not a myth; it is a fact. But instead of dying we are here. The human race lives on because someone is watching over us.

The story of Noah is a story of the wickedness in the human heart that leads to untold evil. But it's also a story of life and how precious life is. The story tells of a loving God who chose to protect life even though only one was truly righteous. This isn't for entertainment. This is a story of who we really are. It's a story that tells us how capable we are of evil but also how we are capable of great righteousness. It's the story of a loving God who saves. And it's a story of what God truly wants from us. Learn the real story.

- In his name -

A Study in "Out of the Saltshaker and into the World"

In 1980, two scientists made an interesting finding in a layer of rock. About 90 million years ago, at just about the time the dinosaurs died off all over the world, a layer of rock was being formed. These two scientists found this layer, tested it, and found it contained a large amount of iridium. Iridium is very rare on earth. It is found mostly in meteorites. This seemed like a huge coincidence that rocks would be filled with iridium just about the time the dinosaurs died, which eventually led these two scientists to an interesting theory; perhaps it was meteors that killed off the dinosaurs.

These two scientists presented their findings to the scientific world, and most scholars rejected this theory at first. Today this theory is accepted as fact by the overwhelming majority of scientists around the world. Imagine where our scientific understanding of dinosaurs and the world might be right now if scientists had continued to reject this theory without giving it any real scrutiny.

We've begun an important book study at Macon Church. The author writes that one event in her life came when she was challenged with the notion that to accept Christianity blindly is a form of "intellectual suicide." The author surprised her skeptical friend by agreeing that accepting any idea blindly is foolish. But she also challenged her friend to consider the other possibility; that by rejecting Christianity without a genuine investigation, she was the one being intellectually blind.

So many people reject the notion of Jesus without giving Christianity a serious thought. People say all sorts of things, many of them negative, about Christianity. What do they really know? How would they know what is true or false when they have never investigated Christianity's claims, or even taken a glance at the Bible? The resurrection is undoubtedly either the greatest truth or the greatest lie in history. Doesn't it deserve close scrutiny and serious investigation? Rejecting the resurrection wholesale is intellectual suicide and possibly far more.

What the world needs is for real people to take a real look at the facts and make an intelligent, educated, choice as to what they really believe. There are plenty of highly intelligent, highly educated people, in the world today that do not reject Christianity. In fact there are scientists and thinkers are now accepting the notion of God as factual. And many other great minds are exploring Jesus with eyes wide open.

Christianity is not some kind of "brain dead" religion; it is a great way of life that can be stimulating to both the heart and mind. It is the great truth that the human heart longs for. It is not something to be rejected lightly but explored and embraced.

So, do what many great minds do; think, learn, explore. Pick up your Bible sometime, read it, and really think about what it's trying to say. You may find yourself uncovering the great truths of life that you've been looking for all your life. Christianity is for the wise and learned, not just the "foolish" or "intellectually blind". Christ is for you.

{The book referenced above is, "Out of the Saltshaker & Into the World: Evangelism as a Way of Life" by Rebecca Manley Pippert}

A Precious Gift

Let's try an experiment. Hold your empty hand out with the palm up. Now imagine if Jesus himself were to appear in your room and offered to put one of three things you're your hand; a check for $10 million, a glass ornament that belonged to someone very special to you, or a vial containing a vaccine that can prevent AIDS or cancer. I am quite certain most people would accept one of these gifts. Which one you would take doesn't really matter; what you would do with it is what matters today.

If you took the check, what would you do? I imagine you'd grip onto it with an "iron fist" and charge to the bank as fast as possible. If you took the glass ornament, you'd probably very carefully carry it someplace safe and take extra special care of it. If you took the vaccine, you'd probably take it to the hospital or some medical researcher to save lives.

The point of this example is if you were to hold something in your hand, something important, something precious, something valuable, it would probably influence you and your behavior almost immediately. You aren't necessarily a good or bad person for selecting the item you chose; you are simply a person who knows a good thing when you've got it.

Christians are not necessarily any better or worse than other people, we are simply people who know a good thing when we've got it. Christians hold onto something very special, very valuable, and very important; the word of God. And when you hold onto something so precious it will alter your behavior and, in fact, alter your very life.

Are there some people reading this article who feel they are not "good people"? I'd like to place a gift into your heart. I want to give you something special, something precious, something important, and something very worthwhile. I want to give you God's word because I know it is a good thing and I believe it will not only change your behavior for the better, I believe it will change your very life. I believe by holding God's word in your heart you can be changed, you can be made into a far better person, and you can have a far better life than the one you have right now.

This isn't about being some kind of religious nut or a "Jesus Freak." It's not about church. This is all about someone giving you a good thing. You know a good thing when you see it. Why not grab onto this good thing and make it part of your life today? Here's a challenge for you; try God for 6 months. Spend a little time every day praying, reading some scripture, maybe reading a devotional (like "The Upper Room" or "Daily Bread"), and go to church every Sunday (It's just an hour a week). Find someone to be your "prayer partner" or "Church Buddy" and talk with them. Just try this for 6 months. If you don't like it, you can always drop it. (How many pastors have ever told you that?)

Try God and God's word for yourself. God is a great friend, always available to talk. God is a great therapist and he works for free. God is a great guide, who leads people to some great new things. Give God a try and see what great things God can bring to you.

One Last Word About Christmas

(An article I wrote a little after Christmas one year.)

Is it too late to be in a Christmas mood? I hope not. Part of the fun of Christmas is to keep the joy going. So, before we put away all our decorations and gifts, I'd like to share a little something I learned this holiday season.

It was around the year 270 A.D. that a man named Nicholas was born in Myra; a city in modern day Turkey. It was during this time that Christianity was illegal, and the Roman Empire would arrest, torture, and even execute Christians. That did not stop Nicholas from converting to Christianity and eventually becoming the Bishop of the church in Myra. Nicholas was a kind and loving man, known as a very Christ-like person.

For this, Bishop Nicholas suffered greatly. He was arrested and tortured for his faith. But he never gave up his hope of being free and being able to worship Christ openly. One day, this came to pass. The Emperor Constantine the Great converted to Christianity and Nicholas was set free.

The stories of St. Nicholas abound. Although there is no direct evidence of it, it is believed Nicholas was present at the council of Nicea, where the early church fathers gathered together the books, we now call The New Testament in our modern bibles. So St. Nicholas may have played an important part in helping to create the church as it is today.

Of course, what Nicholas is best known for are his acts of kindness and generosity. One story is about a man with three daughters who could not afford a dowry for them to marry. (Without a proper dowry, in that age, these girls might never marry.) So, one morning, three bags of money were found in their home. Everyone knew who did it, but no one saw him do this kind deed. Other stories involve Nicholas wearing a disguise and giving gifts to children, feeding the hungry, and helping the sick.

Over the centuries the legend of St. Nicholas has grown and gone through many transformations. The most well-known of course is our modern-day Santa Claus. (Santa is derived from the word for Saint.)

I write this article because I am aware that many churches are often questioning how big a role Santa Claus should play in our modern Christmas celebration. I say, it's time for us as Christians to reclaim our Saint Nicholas. In a nation where so many people believe in the separation of Church and State, and where so many non-believers are offended by religious images appearing in public, I have bad news; you've been honoring a Christian Saint for centuries.

Saint Nicholas was known as a very Christ-like person, and, much like Christ, he has come into a world where the world does not really recognize him. So I say let us Christians honor our old saint, the way millions of others honor him. And let us not be afraid to tell the true story of Saint Nicholas; the story of a man who became loving and giving because he first gave his life to Christ.

In Jesus' Name.

Independence Day 2010

According to a recent survey, a very large percentage of our nation's teens and young adults have no idea what the Fourth of July is all about. They don't understand that a little over 200 years ago, 13 colonies existed on the west coast of North America. These colonists were under the control of the King of England, and he began to oppress the English citizens who lived in these colonies.

So, in 1775, people throughout these 13 colonies began to fight against British troops. On July 4, 1776, the First Continental Congress wrote a Declaration of Independence and voted to go to war with Great Britain. This was a monumental undertaking. The colonies had no navy and no organized army. They were going to war against the greatest Empire in the world at that time. But somehow these colonies overcame the impossible odds and began the nation that we are today. These are well known facts.

Here are some other facts many people do not know.

-When the war was over, people asked George Washington how he beat the British, and his reply was "divine providence". The odds had been so overwhelmingly against him, that Washington believed it had to be God's will for these colonies to win and become a new nation. (And as we study the Revolution we see some unusual events that saved the cause. Events so unusual and so amazing they do seem to be miraculous.)

-When writing the Constitution for this new country, the Founding Fathers felt the need to pray for God's guidance numerous times. So, there were many prayer times in independence hall in Philadelphia.

-The U.S. Constitution contains the words, "We hold these truths to be self-evident, that all men are created equal, that they are endowed by their Creator with certain inalienable rights...."

-All 50 States have a State constitution, and every State constitution, including Michigan's, refers to God or Creator.

-Since 1789, a chaplain or pastor has opened every session of congress with prayer. And, this chaplain is paid with your tax dollars.

-In 1800, as Congress was moving into its new capital building in Washington D.C. it was decided that the capital building would act as a church on Sundays. Many of our Founding Fathers worshipped God in the capital building every Sunday.

And the list of Gods influencing our nation goes on and on. There may be a separation of church and state in our constitution, and it is beneficial to our country, but that does not mean God was excluded from our nation or our form of government. Acknowledging our need for God's guidance has a long and powerful history in our nation and our government.

I write these things because, aside from forgetting what the fourth of July all is about, we are forgetting who we are as a nation. God is very much a part of this country. Religious beliefs led many immigrants to our shores; religious teachings helped to build our government and our constitution; religious faith has been a guiding force in our nation from the beginning. And if a nation forgets where they came from, who they are, and who they are supposed to be, that nation will find itself dying.

America has always been a nation under God. I do believe our nation has been blessed by God many times, and in many ways.

If we don't begin to remember that, and appreciate that, what will the future of our nation be?

Let's take some time this summer to appreciate the summer sun, but also to appreciate who we are as a nation, the God who helped guide our nation, and the God who wants to guide us forward into the future.

And the Angels Danced

Inspired by the Aurora Borealis, 11:30 PM, Tuesday August 26, 1998.

I walked to the lakeshore so I could see,
> a dance of angels in the dark of the night.

It started so simple, so plain to see.
> Just one great finger of light,
> that gently and serenely crept across the sky.

It moved so slowly, hard to perceive, and began to part the curtains;
> curtains of light that would open the passage from heaven.

A dazzling angel, of white and blue, burst forth from the sky in brilliance.
> He spread his wings and cast his splendor across the stars.

Ever so slowly they spread, and the sky was filled with his wings,
> and the light began to shimmer up and down the length of his flowing white robe.

He crossed the sky and looked down upon the great lake.
> And the clouds sang with joy, and the lightning applauded the coming of his glory.

Tongues of red and green flame danced beneath the angel's wings as he gently spread his wonder upon the water.

The lake basked in his beauty, and the waves slapped joyously upon the shore.

Then came the second angel, as if from nowhere, and moved to greet his friend,
and the two angels danced with joy, as fire ripped across the sky.
So great was their display that even the stars began to quiver with joy.

The two moved out across the great waters and walked upon the clouds.
And the flashes of lightning crashed hard into the lake, in appreciation of their grandeur.

Then a myriad of angels came and danced and jumped and ran with glee.
They beat their wings throughout the air, and the heavens pulsed with power.

Thousands of angels came to play and tell the world of God's great love.
The heavens jumped with joy, as the angels danced and jumped and ran and leaped,
and fire burned and glowed and pulsed across this solemn night.

Oh my soul, how great is the Lord.
Oh my soul, how wondrous is the night.

Iron Teeth

Written 1/23/1992

Look at my face, what do you see?
   A beaming smile, joyous as can be?

Beware the smile, a deceiving grin
   It helps to hide the pain that's within.

I have a bright smile, that is no sin,
   But my teeth are iron, to cage feelings within.

Someone hurt me, so long ago,
   But I can't let those feelings show.

Don't show anger, don't get mad.
   Put on a smile, be happy, be glad.

I hate to hurt; I don't want pain.
   Put on a smile, be happy again.

Feelings are strange, a mystery to me.
   Help me to understand, help me to see.

Look past the smile, don't see a fool,
   See a young man, lacking a tool.

How can I deal with passion and pain?
   What can I do so the real man can reign?

Help me break through the false Iron grin.
   Help people to see the man who's within.

A Life in Christ

So many folks are telling me which way I ought to go.
So many voices call to me to leave the path I know.

"Come join us, come try our way, we've got the truth you need."
No you don't, 'cause I've been taught, your voice I should not heed.

Why should I look to moon or stars to see what lies ahead?
I look to the one who made those stars; God leads the path I tread.

Why should I bow and worship the earth, "the mother of us all"?
I look to God, the mighty one, who will never let me fall.

Why caste spells and magic chants to make my life complete?
The greatest magic is Jesus Christ. I kneel at his feet.

"Worship Satan", some have said, "let evil be your goal."
Satan is a liar, prince of death, who'll terrorize your soul.

"Seek enlightenment, do good deeds, your morals can set you free".
I turn to Jesus, greatest of all, who paid the price for me.

He carried a cross of death and pain, so I no longer bear,
The pain and toil of all my sins, my soul's own painful snare.

By his great power and unyielding love, Christ is the victor now.
My own strength was not enough, so to the Lord I bow.

He lifted me up from my own pain, set my feet on the path of life,
so that I can go to tell the world there's freedom from our strife.

My God is mighty, my God has power, a strength beyond compare.
A power Jesus brought to us, so we can freely share.

I need no stars, nor spells, nor devils, nor enlightened ideas old.
My own strength and values and morals and ideals are now like icy cold.

Christ has won the victory, he's master of earth and sky,
He lived among us as a friend, and for our sins he died.

So unto Christ I bring my praise, I give my heart and all.
In Jesus name I live my life, he'll never let me fall.

Techno Terror

(written 7/23/1999. Dedicated to Y2K Hysteria)

The world is headed for a fiery doom,
    Our planet shall face her final tomb.

Cataclysmic disaster is close at hand,
    No escape from Satan's plan.

All because of technology's error,
    Soon the world decay's in terror.

Someone made a computer glitch,
    Now the Earth begins to twitch.

I hear a ticking, soon the time
    For death's own clock is about to chime.

"The end is near," some have said.
    Oh stupid mortals, you've lost your head.

Techno Terror comes near us
    And Chicken Little starts to fuss.

The sky is falling once again,
    Brains fall out and IQs drain.

Earth has been through far worse clips,
    Now we're doomed by microchips?

"I think not," the wise men say,
    "We all have seen worse shades of gray."

Wise is he who knows to pray,
    And puts no faith in computer relay.

In other words-

    Y2K, go away, Come annoy me some other day.

Is There A God?

Genesis 1:1-5; Genesis 6:5-8;Genesis 8:1-4

Is There a God? Unless the answer is yes then everything else we say is kind of pointless. People have believed in something pretty much from the beginning of humanity. But atheism is not exactly new. There have been atheists for centuries. But it has only been in the last 100 years or so that science has made some huge leaps forward that have given people strong scientific reasons to doubt the existence of God.

Today people are not just denying faith but ridiculing believers. Many say believers are foolish, naïve, superstitious, and, of course, having "blind faith." It is foolish to believe simply because we were told to believe it.

For some people that is true. Some believe because it's what they were taught as children and that's all there is to it. But is that the only reason to believe in God? Or is there more to reality than mindless, blind luck.

Today lets examine God from a critical perspective. Let us look for God with our minds, our intelligence, and with logic. Are there intelligent reasons to believe in God.

The God of Science

Let's start with science. Is science the enemy of religion? For most of history it hasn't been. Newton, Einstein, Galileo, and even Charles Darwin did believe in God. For some people throughout history religion was a motivating force to explore, study and think. Although many scientists today are atheists or agnostics, not all of them are. Many scientists proclaim our universe is a beautiful balance of forces and scientific laws that may be indicative of an intelligence at work. Many talk about the complexity of life as proof of a greater mind. And there are an abundance of reasons to proclaim that our existence is proof of a creator.

In the beginning something happened.

Scientists all agree the universe has not always existed as it is. Our universe had a beginning. Where did it come from?

Science tells us, "In the beginning there was a big bang." What is a big bang? That's complicated. To make it simple there was once one tiny dot of reality, perhaps some kind of super black hole, and somehow this dot "exploded." In a fraction of a second matter and energy went flying in all directions and eventually these pieces became the universe we have today.

That is supposedly the beginning. But this beginning does not answer the age-old question that has haunted both atheists and believers for centuries; what came before that? Both sides have always crashed into the same wall. If God made the universe then what came before God? And if there is no God, and we started with a Big Bang, then what came before the Big Bang? And before that, and before that…

Stephen Hawking offered an interesting hypothesis. He argued time was born at the big bang therefore there really is no such thing as "before the Big bang," because without time there's no such thing as before.

I hope people won't accuse me of trying to upstage Stephan Hawking, but I came up with a somewhat similar argument years ago. According to science, the universe is made of energy, matter, and something called space/time. Space and time are not two different things. Somehow they are one thing. Einstein and research have proven that is not just a concept; time is real. So Stephan Hawking's argument can also apply to God; if God made the universe then God made time, and without time there is no such thing as before God. God exists outside of what we would call time.

To believe in God requires faith. That in fact is the essence of religion. And whether scientists want to admit it or not, they sometimes have to take a leap of faith themselves. To believe there is a God takes faith. And to believe the universe was created by accident also takes faith.

When it comes to the beginning, the big point to remember is, even science requires faith sometimes. And as long as we need faith then there will always be room for God.

Now, if scientists are right and the universe was made in a "Big Bang," then there is something we need to remember:

Big Bangs are Messy.

In the beginning there was some kind of super explosion. What happened after that? Scientists believe all the laws of science that govern our universe today were probably created within minutes, if not seconds, after the big bang. The sun shines and the snow falls today because of scientific laws that were made in a flash about 14 billion years ago. And since big bangs are messy most scientists agree it would have been extremely easy for the big bang to have behaved differently, and if it had been different, even slightly different, then the laws of science would be very different than they are.

For example: Water is essential for all life as we know it, and it would probably be important for almost any kind of life we can imagine. Water is made when two atoms of hydrogen lock on to one atom of oxygen at an angle of 104.5 degrees. This happens because of the laws of science.

What if the laws of science were just a little different? What if the hydrogen atoms hooked on to oxygen at a different angle?

What if the hydrogen atoms were separated by a 180-degree angle? Or maybe a 90-degree angle? If that happened water might not behave the way it does. What if water didn't dissolve things very well? Being able to dissolve things is one reason why water is so important for life. What if hydrogen didn't bond very tightly to oxygen? Then water molecules might fall apart. If there was no water, or if water behaved differently, then life would be impossible.

Another law of our universe is gravity. Gravity doesn't just keep us glued to the ground. Gravity is what makes a star into a nuclear reactor by pulling hydrogen atoms together. Gravity keeps earth in orbit. What if the law of gravity was slightly different? If gravity was weaker the sun might be a big, cold, blob of hydrogen. If gravity was stronger then planets, like earth, might not hold their orbits and fall into the sun. If gravity were stronger, or weaker, life may not be possible.

Earth has an electro-magnetic field that protects life from radiation and cosmic rays. If magnetism behaved differently then we might have no protection.

The main point to remember is this; the big bang was so chaotic it's easy to imagine the laws of science being very differently. If the laws of science were just slightly different then life would be impossible. But our universe is arranged and balanced in such a beautiful way that life happens. You might say we live in the "Goldilocks universe," Gravity is not too strong, it's not too weak, it's JUST RIGHT.

Life is never simple.

Something else that is essential to life is DNA. DNA is the blueprint of how to make a living thing. It's made up of amino acids that link together and form something that looks kind of like a twisted ladder. We know nature can make amino acids without help. We've proven that. But even a lot of scientists and skeptics are forced to agree that DNA is far too complicated to have just happened by accident.

If that's true, then either it is created by an intelligence, or the first life must have been something else. One theory is that life was formed from RNA. DNA is like a twisted ladder of proteins. RNA is more like a chain of amino acids. It's a lot simpler and again we've proven nature can make something similar to RNA.So it may be possible that the first life on earth might have been based on something like RNA, or perhaps some other "simple" life, and this simple life eventually evolved into DNA based life. That is logical.

But there is at least one problem with this theory; I've never heard of anyone discovering any RNA based life. If it did exist then where did it go? It all died? That seems unlikely since life has this tendency to keep living. Life adapts, rolls with the punches, evolves, and finds a way. But somehow there is no more simple life left on earth? That seems odd.

In reality there is no such thing as "simple life." Even the simplest known life on earth is rather complex, and rather amazing. Life is hard to make but somehow it exists.

Regardless of how life started, once we have life the story can continue. Some people may not like to hear this from a pastor but if I'm going to stand in the pulpit I must speak the truth. I have done some study on evolution and I believe the theory is quite sound. In fact we see micro evolution all the time. One hundred years ago bacterial infections killed many people. Then one day someone invented penicillin and bacteria found itself on the ropes. But today we are facing a crisis in health care because many bacteria have become resistant to antibiotics. This happened because micro-evolution is real. Life forms survive by changing, adapting, and turning into something new. Micro-evolution is an undeniable fact. So evolution could have taken one celled creature and, after hundreds of millions of years, turned them into some amazing animals and maybe even human beings.

Surviving Disaster.

But for our ancestors to have survived they had to face many obstacles. One of them would have been large and hungry lizard monsters that we call dinosaurs. Human beings would have been lunch if we were walking among Allosaurus, Gorgosaurus, Tyrannosaurus, and others. Our survival might have been impossible.

But then, one day, the dinosaurs all disappeared. Some kind of super disaster, a big meteor, killed off the dinosaurs and opened the door for something else. Was this just a coincidence or is there some greater intelligence out there that had plans for the earth other than dinosaurs?

Now, consider this. What if a meteor had landed right on top of our ancestors when we still lived in one rather small area? Or what if some other super disaster, or deadly disease, had come upon our ancestors? Then we would have gone just like the dinosaurs.

In fact the Bible tells us something pretty terrible did happen a few thousand years ago. According to the Bible God saw humanity had become very wicked, in fact too wicked, So God and wiped out **almost** all humanity but enough were left to allow us to start again.

Science and logic tell us that the Noah story could not be possible in every detail but we do know there were incredible floods in the past. People saw the black sea rise at a phenomenal rate thousands of years ago. When the ice ages ended there were huge floods. For anyone witnessing events like this it must have seemed like the end of the world was at hand.

But flood or no flood science does tell us something did happen that threatened humanity.

About 75,000 years ago a super volcano, kind of like Yosemite Park, exploded. They call it the **Toba Catastrophe**. Millions of tons of rock and dust were blown into the air. The earth underwent a long period of cooling that was kind of like a winter that lasted 6-10 years. For 6-10 years food would have been very scarce. It would have been hard to survive. In fact, according to geneticists after this 6-year winter ended the world contained only 1000-10,000 women and young girls, and some say there may have been less than 1000. These girls and women would become the mothers of us all. That might sound like a lot, but it really isn't. The human race came pretty close to being extinct 70,000 years ago. But, once again, here we are.

Perhaps we should look at the story of Noah in a different way. Maybe it's not a tale of an angry God destroying humanity. Maybe the story of Noah is an ancient memory, passed down for centuries, that once there was a very real event that almost wiped us out. We were almost eliminated but we weren't. Maybe someone stepped in and saved humanity.

There is more that I could say about science, but the fact is there are a few million reasons we should not exist. There are scientists who believe that since our universe is so beautiful, so elegant and so well balanced that it makes life possible, then maybe there is some kind of intelligence in our universe. Not all scientists are atheists and even the atheists have to take a leap of faith sometimes. In some ways that makes the hostility between atheists and believers very unfortunate, because:

Science is not the enemy of God.

If we think of the universe as a house that God made, then what is science? Science is studying the bricks, the plumbing and the electricity. Science is trying to figure out what the wires do, or why the roof keeps the rain out. That is science! If science sometimes comes to a conclusion that seems to contradict the bible, **so what**? Science doesn't exist to verify or deny the bible. Science exists for us to learn and study and to serve humanity. The reason we have so many amazing inventions is because someone did some thinking and some research. God didn't give us a large brain so we could ignore facts and reality. God expects us to learn, explore, and especially think.

Science, logic and thinking are gifts from God, not tools of the devil. We should embrace them, explore the possibilities, learn something new, and see beyond what you already believe. God is far more than you know, far more than you believe, and if we seek for truth, we will find God.

I know for some people the theories of the Big Bang and evolution are problematic. Should they be?

Some years ago someone posed the question to me, "What do you think about evolution?" I had to pause for a moment and think, and I feel like God put the answer into my heart. I said, "Science can tell me where I came from. God tells me what I am." I'm not threatened by evolution. If science wants to tell me I'm an ape, so what? With God in my life and Jesus in my heart I am more than a monkey. I am a child of God.

The God of History

For the people of Israel, seeking God through the use of science was unnecessary. They knew God from their past and from their experience. God was revealed to them and God became their history. Who they were, where they came from, what they believed, and how they became a nation, were all gifts from God. These things were the evidence for God. God was guiding them, step by step, in the past, in the present, and into the future.

There is no question that the most important story in the history of Israel, and the most important story of the Old Testament, is the story of the Exodus. The people of Israel were slaves in Egypt and God used Moses to lead them out of Egypt and make them into a nation. I have 3 movies at home that make great arguments, based on facts and evidence, that the Exodus story was not a myth but is in fact very real and probably very accurate. (The movies are "The Search for the Real Mount Sinai," "Exodus Revealed" and "Exodus Decoded.")

One of the most important parts of the Exodus story is that the people came to Mount Sinai. There they saw the very presence of God as a great fire on the mountain.

There is a mountain on the Sinai Peninsula that has been called the mountain of God but there is ample evidence that it is not the real mountain. Instead, if you follow the bible like a roadmap it leads you to the western side of Saudi Arabia. There we find a mountain called Jabal Al-Lawz and there are strong reasons to think it could be the real Mount Sinai.

Moses heard from God when he was tending the flocks of his father-in-law, who was a priest of Midian. Midian was located on the western side of what is now Saudi Arabia.

The Bible says the mountain of God was the tallest. Jabal Al Lawz is the tallest mountain in the area.

And the Bible says there was a great fire on the mountain. The top of Jabal Al Lawz is black, as if burned by a fire. It is illegal for outsiders to approach Jabal Al Lawz, but a few people claim they have and they claim when they examined the rocks on the top of the mountain. These rocks appear to have been burned black by fire.

Is it just a coincidence that the tallest mountain in the area is black on top? And where could that fire have come from? That does not sound like a natural event. There had to be something else at work.

If the story of Exodus is true, or even just largely true, it is powerful evidence that not only is there a God, but that God has intervened in human history. God changed the direction of the world.

But this is not the only history.

About 700 years after the Exodus the Assyrian Empire invaded Northern Israel, killing and conquering many people, then set their sights on Judah and the southern kingdom. Soon they had crushed almost all the towns and cities in northern Israel then turned their sights on Jerusalem. The Assyrians laid siege on Jerusalem to starve them out. If Jerusalem had fallen it probably would have been the end of their faith. Most religions die when the nations that created them die.

But the prophet Isaiah told King Hezekiah the Lord would deliver them. Sure enough, the bible says an angel of the Lord went into the Assyrian camp and killed thousands in one night. People will doubt the story of the angel, but it is a fact that almost all of the cities and towns on Israel were conquered but Jerusalem somehow survived. God gave them the chance to rebuild the nation and the faith.

About 100 years later the Babylonian Empire invaded Israel and they succeeded in crushing the country and Jerusalem. Thousands of people were dragged away into exile in Babylon and the people left behind lost their temple and began to lose sense of who they were. This also should have been the end of the faith. But soon after Babylon crushed Israel, the Persians invaded and crushed the Babylonians. About 70 years after the Babylonian invasion the King of Persia allowed Nehemiah and others to return to their homeland and they began to rebuild their nation.

It is an incredibly rare event in history that a nation is destroyed and then reborn. How often does it happen twice?

Around 64 BC Rome took control of Israel. After about 100 years of dealing with these troublesome Jewish people the Romans destroyed Jerusalem, destroyed the temple of God and scattered the people around the Roman Empire and beyond. The nation of Israel was done.

But again the faith of the Jews survived, and one day the impossible happened.

More than 1800 years after the fall of Jerusalem, Jewish people from around the world were allowed to return to the land and they began to restore their nation once again. This was impossible but it happened. It looks like there is a God who decided there is something significant about these Jewish people, so God worked a wonder.

But ancient history and Israel are not the only places where we might find God at work.

In more modern history people who would be known as pilgrims came to North America. To make a long story short there were a few dozen things that should have made the great success at Plymouth Rock impossible. The Mayflower almost sank. Storms blew the ship off course off course. By the time the pilgrims arrived it was too late to plant crops. They didn't know how to find food in North America. Disease ravaged the people. The pilgrims should have died.

But the storms blew them off course to an area where a native tribe had recently been wiped out by a disease. The storm brought them to a place where there were fields ready to plant and no one to plant them. The decimation of the tribe caused other nearby tribes to see the land as cursed. in That fear protected the pilgrims from hostile neighbors far better than any wall. And the Pilgrims just happened to find a native American who spoke English, so they were able to make a treaty with their neighbors and make a time of peace and cooperation.

The story of the pilgrims should have gone down in history as a dead end if it was remembered at all. Instead it was a major event in the foundation of America. The story of the Pilgrims is a story where the odds were so greatly against them that it would have taken a miracle for them to succeed. A miracle happened at Plymouth Rock. And there is no question it is a historic event. It is not some fable from some ancient holy book. This story was very real.

I know many native Americans and historians don't see the arrival of Pilgrims as a great miracle, but the fact is the white man was coming whether the indigenous people liked it or not. One of the lessons we should have learned at Plymouth Rock was people who are very different can work together, and even love one another. If people had learned that and lived that lesson the story of America would have been so much different.

Then there are other unlikely historical events that occurred and helped to make America what it is.

In 1755, a young man named George Washington fought for the British in the French and Indian War. He was a colonel, serving under General Braddock. After one intense battle near the Monongahela river Washington returned to camp and looked at his coat. There were four bullet holes in his coat, but not a mark on his body. He should have died right then and there, but somehow he lived to fight in a far more important war. And there were other occasions when Washington had a close call but he survived. Was he just lucky or was he blessed?

In 1775, Washington and others went to war against England. The odds of the colonists winning were incredibly small. There were many reasons the colonists could not have won the war. But it happened and George Washington is perhaps the biggest reason why. George Washington was one of the few generals in history who won a war after losing almost every battle. He was retreating far more than attacking. Very few other people could have lost one battle after another and kept their army together, much less won the war, but somehow he pulled it all together and won a great victory.

In fact, more than once, the revolution was as good as lost.

In August of 1776 Washington was fighting with the British in New York and he was defeated. He had to retreat and soon found himself and 9000 men trapped against the East River. The British General ordered ships to sail up the river and block him in while he prepared for battle. There would be no escape. And once the British captured Washington and his 9000 men it would have been a loss the colonists could not have recovered from. The war was as good as over.

However, the British ships did not block him in. There was no wind that night. Washington had a slim chance to use whatever boats he could find to evacuate. The men worked as fast as they could but as the sun started to rise a large number of his men were still in Brooklyn.

Suddenly a heavy fog set on the area **after the sun rose**. The British army did not advance through the fog and Washington found barely enough time to withdraw everyone. What should have been the end of the war turned into a chance for recovery.

Was it just a coincidence that there was no wind that night to bring ships up the river? Was it just a coincidence that a thick fog rose up on the same night that there was no wind for the ships to sail? Fog usually forms in the night and dissolves as the sun rises. This fog rolled in after the sun began to rise. How often does that happen? Was it coincidence was it divine intervention?

This would not be the only unusual event that saved the Revolution. And if Washington had failed what would have happened to America? And if American history was very different what would world history be today?

In 1917 something very frightening came into the world; Communism took over Russia. People feared communism and with good reason. In the 1950s, nuclear weapons came along it looked like the end of the world was at hand. There were people predicting the end of the world and it did almost happen. A lot of people don't know but Russia and America came close to launching an all-out nuclear strike more than once. We came within an inch of wiping out humanity several times.

But then, just 70 years after the Russian revolution, the Berlin wall came down. Communism began to crumble. In the 1970s nuclear holocaust was practically a certainty. Instead, the threat was over and new hope for the world was born.

Maybe some Pilgrims eating turkey, or a few bullet holes, or a strange fog are not proof that there is a God, but there are many other unlikely events throughout history that have led us to where we are. We are alive, we are still here, and there is hope for freedom and peace eventually. There are many reasons to look at history and believe someone has our back.

The God of Miracles

Are there miracles? Do things happen we cannot explain by any means other than God?

Some people say the existence of life itself is a miracle. Some would see the rebirth of Israel as an act of God. And although the events that protected the pilgrims and George Washington appear to be natural events they were so unlikely and timed so perfectly they at least border on the miraculous.

Over the centuries there have been many events that defy logical explanation, even with modern investigation. There have been miraculous healings that are well attested to. There are people who have demonstrated abilities that science cannot explain. When I was considering what miracles to talk about, I found myself with several to consider. Which one should I use?

One that is rather well known and well attested to took place in Fatima, Portugal 1917. Three children supposedly saw the Virgin Mary in a tree near their home. Mary appeared several times and made some predictions.

She promised that on Oct. 13 she would send a sign. Many people showed up to watch. Some people in attendance said it seemed like the sun started falling closer to the earth and that it danced around in the sky.

Whatever really happened that day, the children said Mary made predictions. In one of them she said the war, WW1, was coming to an end but if people did not stop sinning another great war, even more destructive than the first, would occur. She also predicted there would be a great sign the war was near.

"When you see a night illumined by an unknown light, know that this is the great sign given you by God that he is about to punish the world for its crimes, by means of war, famine, and persecutions of the Church and of the Holy Father."

In January 1938, an incredible light, described as a rare Aurora Borealis, was seen from Canada to Bermuda to Austria and to Scotland. It was an unprecedented light display.

On March 12, 1938, Hitler annexed Austria. In September he annexed the Sudetenland. In September 1939, Hitler invaded Poland.

Was this all just a coincidence? Some say so, but it is such an interesting and unlikely set of events it is hard to dismiss it as pure chance.

And there have been many other wonders that have taken place over the centuries. Some can be dismissed because there were few witnesses and poor records, but not all wonders can be ignored. There is evidence that there is far more to the world than any of us will ever understand. There is reason to believe there is a greater reality "out there somewhere."

Conclusions:

I have but hit on a few bits and pieces of evidence that there is a greater consciousness and a higher power in this universe. I could go on, but I know some skeptics will never believe. Some people may find flaws in my science, criticize my history, and outright ridicule me for saying that miracles might exist. But I hope I have made one point very clear:

Religion does not have to be a result of "blind faith."

To believe in God does not have to be the result of superstition, stubborn traditions that refuse to die, or a lack of intelligence. A belief in God can result from logic, critical thinking and even evidence.

Not long ago science found evidence for the Higgs-Boson particle. It has been called "The God Particle." Naturally some people have stated that since we found it we have proof there is no God. I jokingly replied online that in fact the opposite is true because I looked closely at the Higgs-Boson particle and saw the tag that reads, "Made in Heaven." I do not believe I will ever see that day but I don't need to. Religion will always require a leap of faith. But, when we think, study, and learn, we will see that our leap of faith is not as big a leap as some people claim. God is not illogical or an anti-intellectual concept. God is what God is and God is real.

Who was Jesus and Why did he Die on a Cross?

1 John 1:1-2:2; John 1:1-14; Matthew 17:1-9

Once, on a cold Christmas Eve, a farmer was home enjoying a warm fire. His wife and children were off to church, and he was home alone because church was not "his thing".

As he sat by the fire he heard a strange noise coming from outside. He went out into his yard and found a group of small birds sitting in the snow. The farmer knew those poor birds would soon freeze to death if he didn't do something. His barn was nearby, so he went, opened the barn door, and turned on the light. But the birds did not go to the light. So he laid out a trail of food for the birds to follow, but the birds didn't follow the trail. Finally he ran around them and tried to shoo them toward the open barn door, but that just caused the birds to scatter and panic. So he stood there for a moment in the cold, wondering what to do. And the farmer thought to himself, "If only I could become a bird, I could show them the way."

So it is with God. Just as a kindly man **would** become a bird to save some birds if he could, so God **became** a man, to show men and women the way to God.

If you ask 1000 people, "What is God really like?" you may get about 1000 answers. But, ask a Christian that question, and you are supposed to only get one answer; **God is like Jesus**, because God is in Jesus and Jesus is in God.

Was Jesus a man? Most definitely. The Bible is very clear; Jesus was born of a woman. Jesus grew up. Jesus ate food. Jesus slept. Jesus felt pain. Jesus was very much a human.

But the Bible is also very clear, that Jesus was somehow more than human.

"In the beginning was the Word. The Word was with God and the Word was God ... and the Word became flesh..." Although we can debate exactly what these words mean the gospel of John clearly states that Jesus existed from the beginning of time. Through Jesus, the entire world came into being.

John used the Greek word Logos when he wrote his gospel. The word Logos does not mean literally mean "Word" or "Word of God." Logos is a Greek belief that somehow underneath our reality there is a greater reality connecting everything together. Think of a field of grass. It looks pretty impressive all by itself. But we all know there is a long stretch of dirt and rock holding each blade of grass close to each other, and this dirt and rock goes down and out for miles and miles. What we see is just the surface. Every planet and every star are just blades of grass. Underneath it all there is one greater reality that holds all these things together.

John is saying that the greater reality is the Word of God, and the Word of God is Jesus himself. The Word of God was one with God from the beginning. And the Word became a person. Somehow God who is greater than all reality walked upon the earth with very human feet: Jesus.

It sounds a little strange. How can people believe this? To Jewish people the idea that somehow Jesus or anyone else could be God on earth was absolute blasphemy. The Bible says there is one God and only one God. You can't have God in heaven and God on the earth in Jesus. You can't somehow divide God or have "partners" for God.

However, not long ago, scientists found a few bodies buried near Jerusalem. Two men, who were apparently Jewish, were buried in the first century and they were buried with tiny scrolls with scripture written on them. This was common practice. However, what was unusual is these scrolls contained a few verses from the gospel of Matthew. Not only does this finding prove that at least some parts of the gospel of Matthew were written earlier than some people believed, but Jesus' name is not spelled out. On these tiny scrolls Jesus is referred to **only by his initials**. In the Bible, only one is referred to only by his initials; God. Apparently, some Jewish people were equating Jesus with God within 70 years of his death.

Whoever wrote these scrolls was not alone. The Jewish Christian Paul wrote to a man named Titus and talked about, "Our God and Savior Jesus Christ."

When Thomas looked at Jesus 10 days after he was supposed to be dead, Thomas said, "My Lord and My God." Something incredible must have happened to cause this unbelievable change in the minds and teachings of Jewish people. People believed God was walking on earth in Jesus Christ.

What does that mean to us today? It means we are the tiny birds lost in the snow, in danger, and we need someone to save us.

We talk of salvation but many will ask, "What do we need to be saved from?"

The philosopher Santayana is credited with saying, "Those who do not remember the past are doomed to repeat it." I wish I could talk to Santayana sometime and tell him, "Sorry, but even when people do remember their history, quite a few of them repeat it anyway." War follows war and injustice follows injustice. One bad decision gets repeated over and over again a thousand times for a thousand years. That is the history of the human race.

Today we live in the wealthiest, most prosperous, nation that has ever existed in human history. There's more than enough food and water for life. We have a great education available (whether we use it or not is another issue) and we have many things to keep us interested and entertained. So why are so many people so miserable? Why is there practically an epidemic of depression, suicide and fear in America? To deal with these troubles many people are turning to self-help books, pop psychology, psychics and others. Churches are suffering while cults and new age groups are growing.

Why? It's the disease of the human soul. It's called sin. Doctors and psychologists perform essential tasks in our modern world. We need them, but they cannot cure the soul. No teacher, no philosopher, and no new age guru can change what we are. Our core never changes **UNTIL** we place our lives and our very selves into the hands of God.

Sin is losing sight of God. Sin is when we walk from God to follow our own way. Sin is us being far from God.

Salvation is getting back to God.

But no matter what we do we can't find our way there. We cannot reach up and grab on to God. So God reaches down and grabs on to us.

God does this by sending Jesus Christ into our world. Jesus came to seek and save the lost. Jesus came to find the sinners and show them the path to God.

And Jesus' job did not end at his death. Jesus is still here, seeking to enter into our lives and into our very hearts and souls. Thanks to Jesus we can lose our "addiction" to sin and start to recover. We become a new creation by letting Jesus into our lives and making us into a new people. Salvation comes when we let ourselves be found.

In Jesus' time many people were sacrificing animals to God to pay the cost of their sins. About 2000 years ago, God provided a real sacrifice for all the people of the world. John 3:16, "For God so loved the world he sent his only son, that whoever believes in him should not perish, but have everlasting life." God gave the world his own Son, knowing how the world would treat him; knowing the world would reject him and even kill him. But by dying on a cross Jesus sets people free from their slavery to sin and gives them a new life.

How does this work? The most common belief today is that we all deserve death for our sins, and God demands justice. By sacrificing animals the sins were paid for in blood. So when Jesus died it was a 1-time, ultimate sacrifice to pay for all the sins of all the world.

This is perhaps the most commonly held belief. But there are actually several explanations for Jesus' death and how it brings salvation.

There's another story about a pastor and some birds. One day, a pastor was walking down the road, when he saw a young boy with a birdcage. In the cage were two wild birds the boy had caught. The pastor asked the boy, "What are you going to do with them?" The boy said, "I'm going to take them home, pull out all their feathers, and kill them." The pastor was rather unhappy to hear that, so he said to the boy, "How much do you want for those birds?" The boy said, "Pastor, you want these birds? They're not pretty; they don't sing really well; they can't be pets. Why would you want them?" The pastor said,

"How much?" The boy said, "Five dollars." The pastor paid the boy, took the cage, and set the birds free.

One day Jesus was walking down a road when he saw the devil carrying a cage. In the cage Jesus saw all the souls of all the people of the world. Jesus asked Satan, "What are you going to do with them?" Satan said, "I'm going to take them, torture them, destroy them, and do all sorts of evil to them." Jesus said, "How much do you want for them?" Satan said, "Jesus, these people aren't worth anything. They kill one another, they make war, they mess things up, and they don't listen to God." But Jesus said, "How much?" And Satan said, "O.K. It will cost you all your pain, all your tears, and all your suffering. You will have to die a horrible death on a cross." And Jesus said, "It's a deal."

The human race is addicted; addicted to sin and evil. Jesus came to break the hold sin has on our lives and make us into a new people. On that horrific yet beautiful cross Jesus brought salvation.

The cross changes us. The cross shows us God's pain, and it also shows us God's love. This is what God has done, for you. And if we really see it that makes a powerful impact.
Still some will keep saying, "There must have been some other way." Well, what if there was another way? What if God could have brought about salvation differently? Then the truth is this; **IF** there was indeed some other way to bring salvation, **IF** there was indeed a less bloody way to save our souls, **THEN** it means Jesus **CHOSE** the cross. Jesus Christ chose crucifixion. Why? Maybe it was the easiest way for us to find salvation. Maybe it was the best way for us. But imagine how powerful it is to consider that Jesus may have had alternatives, but he chose to be crucified for us.

People are willing to make a few small sacrifices to save some birds, some dolphins, some whales. Wouldn't you make a big sacrifice to save your child? Isn't God willing to make a large sacrifice for God's children?

But God's sacrifice is not the end of the story. The Bible teaches us that the wages of sin is death. Since Jesus was God, Jesus was without sin. If Jesus was without sin, then he should not have died. So, the power of sin is broken by Jesus' death, and even the power of death could not hold Jesus. Jesus has broken death and given all of us a chance at eternal life. By dying and rising again, Jesus has made a bridge that stretches from heaven to earth. God walks down the bridge and comes to us, then shows us the bridge to reach to God. Our bridge is Jesus Christ himself.

The story of Jesus is the story of God coming to us to show us the way. God himself has come to earth to bring salvation. A new life, and eternal life, is waiting for all who believe. This is the message of Jesus and this is the message of the cross.

Open your hearts and let Jesus, the crucified, risen and living savior, come into your life and make you a new person.

In Jesus' name.

What is God Really Like?

Genesis 22:1-2, 9-14; Like 15:11-32

There was a man who had some serious personal issues, so he started visiting a therapist. The two of them spend a lot of time together. During one of their sessions the subject of God came up, and the counselor asked him what he thought God was really like? The man thought for a moment and said, "Well, **if** God does exist, he's a mean old man sitting on a porch watching you. He doesn't say much, he doesn't do much, until you make him angry, then you better <u>watch out</u>." And the psychologist thought for a moment and said, "That doesn't sound like God. That sounds like your father."

A lot of experts agree, your first image of God was born the day you were born. There you were, bundled up in a little blanket, looking up at those giants standing around you. Those giants were pretty amazing people. If it was dark they could make light appear. If you cried they put food in your mouth. They picked you up and cuddled you. They were pretty impressive. That's where your idea of God began.

And that can be where people start to develop very flawed images of God. Even if you had good parents, is any human being perfect? Of course not, so your first impressions of God were rather flawed.

So try to imagine what God must look like to people who had a terrible childhood. Imagine what God must look like to someone who suffered abuse as a child. Imagine if your first picture of God was physically abusive, sexually abusive, or emotionally abusive. Imagine if your idea of God was always screaming, drinking or hurting someone. There is no question many children grow up in a home where there is a serious problem.

There are a lot of people out there who say they are not "Big believers". They say God is not all that important to them. This is what people say, but is it true? We all have an image of God buried in the back of our heads somewhere, even if we are not big believers.

Imagine if your God is the Great Abuser in heaven. You may not think about it often but it is always there. What would life be like if you really believed God was a mean old man just waiting to strike you? A life like that would be a life filled with stress. When God's out to get you, life can be very scary.

Why were so many evil things done to black people and Native Americans? Partly because someone said it was, "God's will". Why did hundreds of people follow Jim Jones into the jungle of Guyana and kill themselves? Because that's what he told them God wanted. Why do people strap bombs onto their chests and go blow up other human beings? Because that's their image of God. Whether we want to admit it or not our beliefs about God matter a great deal in our lives.

These are some extreme examples but the same is true for rather ordinary lives and ordinary circumstances. Why are millions of Americans so unhappy? Why are people dissatisfied with life? Maybe because they think God does not love them. When your God doesn't care, life becomes cold.

But that's not God. These are false images of God and that's a lesson we actually should have learned long before Jesus was born.

If you visit Israel you might want to visit the archeological digs at Tel Meggido. Deep beneath the surface archeologists found the remains of civilization that dated from before even the time of Abraham. In the middle of the ruins they have found a large, round, sacrificial altar where people performed human sacrifice.

Nearly 4000 years ago, Abraham lived at a time when some people would literally take their own child, place them on an altar, and sacrifice them to the gods. That was what they felt the gods wanted. So one day Abraham must have looked at the world around him and he probably thought, "If this is what other people do, shouldn't I be willing to do it for my God?" So he took his son, the son he had waited decades to have, and placed him on a makeshift altar. He was about to murder his own son when suddenly the real God showed up, and God said something <u>revolutionary</u>. God said, **"No."** Here was a god said, "That is not what I want." This was really a revolutionary moment in the history of religion. The real God said "No" to human sacrifice. This God said, "I am not a bloodthirsty monster." That took place about 4000 years ago, but some people still aren't listening.

About 2000 years ago Jesus said, "God makes the sunshine on the evil and the good." Isn't that true? Do good people get extra sunshine? Do bad people get a lack of rain? There are times it may feel that way but it's not true. There are people who have been born into misery but was it God who handed them that life, or was it someone else? Doesn't poverty and injustice exist because people create it or at least allow it?

When Jesus talked about God, he usually used a very common, simple image; the father or mother. I believe the story we often call "the prodigal son" may be the most important image of God ever made.

It can be beneficial to give a story a name. It helps us remember it and it comes to mind quickly. The problem with labeling a story, like calling it "the prodigal son," is we think we know what it's all about. Do we? There is a lot more to this story than most of us know.

So, instead of just reading from the Bible, I want to tell a story. "Once upon a time," there was a man who had two sons. One day the younger son said to his father, "Father, I want my share of the inheritance today." This may seem unusual to us, but back then, according to customs, a son could ask for his share while his father was alive. This father agreed. He would have broken his property into three equal parts. He would have kept one part for himself to live on until his death, and then give the other two to his sons.

The older son stayed at home, the good and faithful son that he was. But the younger son took his money and he did the unthinkable; he sold his share of the property. Even though we might say his name was on the deed, it was really family land. It may have been in his family for generations, or perhaps it was land his father worked hard for and purchased. In either case, <u>it was improper to sell part of the family farm while your father was still alive</u>. But this young man did just that. Then he took the money and he left. Not only did he leave his father and brother, he left his country. Faith, family, and the Holy Land have always been of extreme importance to the Jewish people. This boy left it all behind so he could go live a life of "loose living."

In modern terms, you might say the boy ran off to Las Vegas or other wild city and he started throwing away money on drinking, drugs, gambling, parties and prostitutes. Whose money is he spending? He's not spending money he earned himself; he's wasting family money on sinful living. His sins are not only growing, they are compounding.

But perhaps one of his greatest sins is really the sin against himself. What happens to a lot of people who start to live a life like this? They don't just waste their money, or their time, or talents. People start to lose themselves. This young man lost who he was and everything that really matters in life.

Then, one day, the money was gone. Even today there are plenty of people who acquire great wealth and somehow lose it all. Back then it was no different except there was no bankruptcy court or financial expert to get your life back on track. When the money was gone his so-called friends also left. Friends like this are not really friends; they are parasites. When the party's over, they move on.

So, the young man was broke, in a foreign country, no friends, no family, and then you might say a recession came along. There was no welfare system back then, no food stamps, so he started to starve.

Finally one day a farmer hires him to feed the pigs. <u>Jewish people do not take care of pigs</u>. It would be an incredibly demeaning situation for him but he was so desperate he had no choices. He became so hungry even pig food started to look good. We often say you have to hit rock bottom before you start looking up. You can't get much more "rock bottom" than a Jew who thinks pig food looks good. So one day, this young man came to his senses and he decided, "My father has servants who are eating, and I'm starving. I'm going home."

Now, this is where the <u>real</u> danger begins. In the story "Fiddler on the Roof," a Jewish man's daughter runs off and marries a Christian. What happened to the daughter when she married a Christian? Her father said, "She is dead to us." That's not just a movie. It happens today, even here in 21st Century America.

So this boy is headed home and he could be headed for disaster. If this boy arrived in his hometown and people in the town see him first, they could drag him into the center of town and perform a banishment ritual on him. He would be considered dead and no one, not even his own family, would be permitted to talk to him. And even if his father finds him first he had every right to banish him. He could say to him, "You abandoned me, you abandoned your brother, you even abandoned God. You are not my son." In fact some people might argue his father had an obligation to banish him.

So, on the way home, the son rehearses a speech to give his father. "Father, I have sinned against heaven, and against you, I am not worthy to be called your Son, treat me liked a hired servant." Maybe he's not all that sincere but he had better try something.

The story then tells us when this boy is still **a good distance** from the house, his father sees him. A good distance away. What does that mean? Maybe the father has been spending time on the main road, a fair distance from the house, looking for him. Maybe the father has not just been waiting at home. Maybe he has been out and about hoping to find him first.

And when he saw his son, Jesus said he was "filled with compassion." So he ran up to his son and grabbed him. By holding on to him the father is saying to the entire community, "This is my son. I will decide what happens to him." This also means the father is setting himself up for ridicule. People in town will lose a lot of respect for this man if he takes his worthless son back.

(Does that shed a little light on the cross? By letting Jesus be crucified, didn't God set himself up for ridicule?)

So, the son launches into his "rehearsed speech." But the Father says, "Get the best robe in the house, put it on him. Get shoes on his feet, and a ring on his finger." This ring isn't a piece of jewelry. It would have been a signet ring. It has the family seal on it. Only a son, or a very trusted servant, would be allowed to wear the family seal.

Then he tells his servants to get the best meat available and celebrate. "My son was dead, now he's alive. My son was lost, now he's found." The Father knows his son has sinned a great sin, he knows the son's speech may be rehearsed, and he knows he will face ridicule for this. But by welcoming this boy home and putting the ring on his finger, the Father is telling his son, and he's telling the entire world, "This is my son."

This is what God is really like. Once we wake up and realize what a mess our lives have become, once we realize how sinful we are, God is ready to say, "Welcome home, my beloved child." We don't need a long, elaborate ritual; we don't need to go through a painful cleansing process. We just need to come home and God is ready to celebrate. God is the God who wants to put his mark upon our lives, like a signet ring, and say to us, "You are my beloved child." That's what God is really like.

The Bible says God is a God of light and in God there is no darkness at all. The Bible says God is love; God's very nature is all that is pure and good and giving.

Now there is one more character in this story. He is the older son; the good boy who stayed home and has been a good son all his life. When he found out his sinful brother has come home and father is throwing a party for him, he was furious. He refused to join the party, so the father came to him. The father says, "You are my Son, you have always been my son, and I love you. But your brother was lost to us. Your brother was dead, but now he's alive again."

A lot of churches are full of "older brothers;" people who have been faithful, loyal Christians all their lives. Churches, especially older churches, are often full of people who sacrificed a lot to keep the doors open. So when a newcomer comes in the door, especially someone with a bad reputation, some church people are not very welcoming. This story is largely intended for sinners, the people who wandered away from God, but it is also for those who have been good and loyal all their lives. God calls on us to remember that sinners are our brothers and sisters. Human beings' sin, human beings fail, human beings make <u>huge</u> mistakes, but human beings can also be loved, forgiven, and reborn by the power of God. God calls on us to celebrate when a sinner comes home. If you aren't happy when some people come into your church, just remember, there's someone in your church who used to be more like the prodigal son than the responsible brother. And quite often it's your pastor.

God is the good father who wants to grab onto all of us and say to the world, "<u>Excuse me. I believe that I'm God, not you. I will decide what happens to my child.</u>" God is the God who has a big "welcome home" sign waiting for everyone who comes home. God is the God who is ready to throw a party, for you.

In the story, the father finds his son while he's still a long way off. God is not just waiting for you; God is actively seeking you. Jesus told another story about a shepherd who had 100 sheep. One day, he only counted 99. What should the shepherd do? Be happy with 99? No! He went out to find that one that was lost. God is the good shepherd who goes to find even one lost sheep. God is the good father, seeking out each lost child. God is the God who wants life, not death. God is the God who wants to bring healing, not pain. God is the loving father who takes abuse and ridicule for our sake. God cares about sin, but God doesn't want to punish. God wants us to come home. God wants us to be part of God's family again. That's the real God.

You can truly worship God today by starting to put aside false images of God. Those false images are hurting you and they are probably hurting the people around you. People who follow a negative God can be very negative people, and negative people often hurt the ones around them.

Put that false God aside and start grasping onto the real and beautiful God.

Yes, life will still bring you some bad days. But, with the loving and true God in you, life will be a lot better. You will be a lot happier. You will start to see life as you are supposed to see it.

Seek this God. Make this God part of your life. Swallow this God into your whole being, and you will be made whole. This is the real God, who wants to be part of your life, and wants you to be part of the family.

In Jesus' name:

Do I Have to Go to Church?

Acts 2:42-47 and Matthew 18:15-20

There once was a man who one day gave his life to God. He became quite a believer in Jesus Christ, but he would not go to church. Many people came to him, talked to him, tried to convince him that church was important, but he still would not go. So, one day, the pastor from his wife's church came by, and the two men began to talk. The man went on and on about why he felt church was not all that important, that he didn't need four walls and a roof to pray. The pastor said almost nothing during this discussion, he just let the man talk. After a while, the pastor looked over at the fire burning in the fireplace. He took the fireplace poker and pulled one tiny hot burning ember out of the fire and set it on the stones in front of the fireplace. After a very short time the ember cooled and turned black. The pastor reached down with his bare hand, picked up the ember that had been red hot just minutes ago, and handed it to the man. The man took the ember and said, "Thanks for the great sermon pastor." After that he started attending church.

One ember, all by itself, will burn out rather quickly. But, when it's in a group, those embers can keep each other hot, and keep a fire burning, for a long long time.

People have asked me the question, "Why should I go to church?" "Do I need four walls to pray?" "Do I need an organ and stained glass to be a good Christian?"

Well, the piano and the organ weren't invented until hundreds of years after Jesus. The early churches did not have stained glass, and quite a few of them definitely did not have four walls and a roof. Quite a few of the early Christians met in homes, or basements, or out in the woods. Early churches were often illegal organizations. Our Christian ancestors were technically criminals in Rome, engaging in illegal activities, so they had to hide.

Some Christians even met in the catacombs under Rome. Many Roman Christians literally had church services in a tomb. There was no fancy building. There were no fancy musical instruments. What did the early church have? They had one another.

The Greek word in our New Testament that we translate as Church is the word Ecclesia. Ecclesia has nothing to do with a building; Ecclesia means the assembly, or the fellowship; some people might argue it might even mean "the family."

Early churches were people, and that's about all they were. These people met together pretty much wherever they could. They worshipped together, they taught about Jesus, they engaged in acts of charity and they especially loved one another. That is where we started. That is Church in its truest form.

This is how they kept their faith alive.

According to the book of Acts, the Disciples were all together, sharing what they had, giving to the poor, and praising the name of God. Jesus said, "Wherever two or three are gathered in my name, there I am in the midst of them."

Every once in a while, it seems the church forgets that this is where it came from. So, every once in a while, someone has to come along and remind the church of who they are, and what they are supposed to be.

Martin Luther of course is called the great reformer. He saw what he felt was corruption and errant theology in the church and he rebelled against it. He tried to pull the people back to the Bible and the origins of the faith.

What is not so well known is that, at first, Martin Luther was very much in support of small groups of people gathering, reading scripture together and praying for each other. Other reformers also saw the value of small group ministry but because the conditions at the time were so hostile Luther never initiated small groups.

But others did. In the early 16th century John Calvin did a lot of great ministry through small groups.

In the 18th century John Wesley encouraged churches to begin holiness groups; people who would meet for prayer, scripture, and to hold one another accountable to their beliefs. John Wesley was an Anglican Priest who found himself getting rather disillusioned with the Anglican Church. He felt the church was not really attending to the needs of the people, and the church was more interested in having church than in being holy. So he started forming small groups within churches. These groups went by different names, but one name that kind of stuck was the word Methodist. The people who joined these groups made a commitment to dedicate themselves to lives of holiness, prayer, bible and fellowship. This is where the Methodist Church began; small groups dedicated to holiness and building one another up in faith.

If you really want to understand this sermon you might want to pronounce it properly. Try to sound like a whiny little child saying to his mother, "Do I have to go to church?" That's was my voice years ago.

You might say I've been writing this sermon since I was 9 years old. That's when a new pastor came to my home church and I was not a happy person. He was a very nice man and seemed very good at his job. But just about everyone has the exact same criticism of him; he was preaching over EVERYONE'S head. Imagine being 9 years old listening to sermons like that, and many lasted over half an hour. In the middle ages European priests spoke their messages in Latin. As far as I was concerned he may as well have speaking Latin. I hated church.

I believe part of the problem many churches face is they put too much emphasis on the worship service. Yes, Sunday morning service is important, in fact very important, but it is just one part of the church message.

Some of my own best memories as a Christian took place in my college days when I was part of a small fellowship group, IVCF. We met a couple times a week, read scripture, challenged one another to live more holy lives, we did good works for others, and we shared with one another our understanding of scripture and theology.

That should be part of what a church is. Church can be a formal meeting one day with an educated pastor preaching a message, but then we can also meet together with one another, discussing the sermon, sharing the message, sharing our faith and our understanding of what the messages really mean. This can be your church as well. And for some people it might be a far more real experience than the worship service.

Yes, it is a good thing for a person to read scripture and pray alone. Jesus said, "When you pray, don't make a big public production of it. Go into your closet and pray in secret." This is important.

But, when you pray, and you feel God wants you to do something, wouldn't it be a good idea to talk to others and see if they think it's something God would indeed ask you to do?

Wouldn't it be wise to ask them to pray for you and give you guidance as you explore God's will?

Quite a few cults have been started by one person who felt they were right about scripture and didn't listen to anyone else. One of the reasons we have so many denominations is because a few people thought they were right and didn't listen to anyone else. Wouldn't it be wise to gather, talk, share our understanding, and perhaps come to an answer together? If we did that then perhaps we wouldn't have so many denominations and so many problems.

Have you ever found certain scriptures confusing? How will you understand them unless you study and learn AND talk to other people who also have some learning and understanding? These are things you cannot do alone. These are things you can only do in a group. That is Church.

Christianity is not a "one person" religion and it never was. Christianity is a social faith. Christianity is about God and what God does in and through people. You live out your faith with others. You practice your faith with others. You learn new things from others. You share ideas and grow in faith with others. And when you are having a bad day, or two, or a bad year or two, who do you go to? The church is here so **we** can help one another in troubles. We are a group designed to build one another up in faith.

Yes, the church has problems. Evil behavior by certain priests and other clergy pollute our headlines making us all look evil. People do not understand that such perversion is everywhere. Supposedly your pastor is actually less likely to abuse children than many other people in certain professions.

And people are constantly making I disparaging remarks about "organized religion," especially people who have been hurt by organized religion. Years ago a group began called, "Fundamentalists Anonymous." It was for people who felt they'd been emotionally victimized by a church's theology. And there are plenty of other, ordinary, down to earth, issues that can make church an unpleasant and even hurtful experience.

No matter how well intentioned an organization may be, no matter how high its ideals, all organizations are run by people. No matter how hard we try to prevent it we will always bring our issues, personal problems, anger, pride and arrogance with us wherever we go, including into the church. People have been hurt by churches and well-meaning church members. (I have often joked every church would be fantastic if there just weren't people in them.)

Sometimes a church welcomes a pastor who is not very good. Pastors bring their issues and problems with them into the pulpits. That affects the people they are supposed to serve.

And pastors aren't perfect either. We have the same weaknesses as anyone else. Hopefully church members understand this and try to work with their pastors. Instead a lot of people have a tendency to walk out the door. Why? Bad pastors can be removed, and you aren't supposed to be coming to church for a pastor. **You are supposed to come for God, for your own spiritual needs and especially come together for everyone's good.**

Besides, if we do away with organized religion what would we have? Disorganized religion? If we do not find ways to work together as Christians then our faith will be even more of a mess.

Is there anyone in this town that could afford to pave all the roads in this area? No! But if everyone pays their taxes and elects people to lead and organize then the road gets paved and other things get done.

Can one person alone feed all the hungry people in the world? Of course not. But when millions of people, all over the world, put in a few dollars, millions of people get fed. That's what church should be. The church is supposed to be **US**, working together, for the good of everyone. We, the people, are the real church.

If people in church really loved one another, really worked for good, and held tightly to God and each other, then a church would survive a bad pastor, a few disagreements, and even some big fights.

Quite a few people quit church because someone said the wrong thing. That's one person being human; forgive them. Sometimes in church you may see a group of people trying to "take over". Love those people and talk to them before things get out of hand. This is what a church can be.

Church is people. Church is you and me working together for the growth of our faith, for building one another up and for spreading the word.

Church is about everybody, because everyone has a sermon in him or her. The pastor is not the only one who preaches; we all preach in one-way or another every day. What we do and what we say represents God. And we all have a message to share. I read a book one day that says every believer has one sermon in them; a preacher is simply someone who knows how to say his sermon 1000 different ways.

God has put a message into you. God has given you something to say, something to share, and someone out there needs to hear it. My duties are to tell the truth, spread the word, build people up in faith, educate, and help the church to grow. But, guess what? That's your job as well. Church is not a one-man show. Church is a place for everyone to gain faith, share faith, and help others grow in faith. Someone needs to hear your message one way or another.

And you need to hear someone else's message. The pastor is on the pulpit sharing their understanding of scripture, their stories and their beliefs. That's what they are trained to do. But sometimes the pastor needs to hear a good sermon as well. Pastors need some inspiration and spiritual food sometimes. I bet your pastors would love to hear you say, "Pastor, I've got a message I'd like to share. Could I speak it in church some Sunday?" That does not happen in many churches very often. **It should**, because all the people, laity and clergy, have a message to share.

Yes, you have to go to church. One Christian alone is a Christian that can lose their faith and their fire for God very quickly. One Christian alone cannot feed too many hungry people. One Christian alone cannot always understand scripture. Christians need each other

And there won't be Christianity without some kind of organization that we commonly call church. The church won't grow if we aren't working together. People want to be part of a church where there's love and goodness. The world needs to see Christians loving one another and building something good together. And if we can make that kind of church, we can bring people to church and bring people to God.

There's a song child often sing in Sunday School. Perhaps it is a kid's song but sometimes truth can be made known through our children.

"I am the church, you are the church, we are the church together.

All who follow Jesus, all around the world, yes, we're the church together."

The most important thing to remember is that we do need church because we are the church. We gather together for a higher purpose; we gather for God and for the good of all.

In Jesus' name.

Each one a minister

1 Peter 2:1-12; Mark 10:35-45

I believe it was June 28, 1990 that I pulled into the driveway of my first parsonage of my first appointment as a pastor. On that day a man named Bill was there to greet me. He and some others were in the parsonage helping clean up and waiting to greet me. The next day it was Bill who drove me around the churches, showed me where I needed to be and when and showed me around the area. A couple days later it was time for my first Sunday as pastor. That afternoon it was Bill, his mother, and his girlfriend who took me out to lunch, drove me around the area, and helped me get acquainted with my new home.

Over the next couple years I saw quite a bit of Bill because Bill was practically "Mr. Everything" in that church. He was the treasurer, he served on committees, and whenever there was a special service or a special event, Bill was there.

Sadly, during my third year in the church Bill was involved in a tragic car accident. His mother and girlfriend were killed, and Bill was severely brain damaged. He was horribly disabled for the rest of his life. It was after the accident we all learned, the hard way, just how important Bill really was in that church. Aside from what we all saw him do he did a lot of other good things behind our backs. There are several very valuable lessons to learn from his life. One of them no church should ever let one-person handle so much responsibility alone. After the accident the church was seriously handicapped.

But there is another, far more positive, lesson to learn. One day I was having some troubles as pastor. The church was not growing, and I was feeling rather down about it. I talked with someone who said I was beating myself up for a lot of things.

That's when he said to me, "Lance, you can't do it all alone. Don't the church members have something to do with the church growing or not? What if everyone in your church was like your best member?"

I said to him, "If everyone in my church was like Bill, I'd probably be unemployed. They wouldn't need a pastor."

As I look back over my years as pastor, I recall many members who really stood out. I recall several people who went that extra mile, or 2, or 3, for their church. I recall people who were "the glue" that held the congregations together.

Truly I tell you, if every single person who attended a church was like Bill, or some of the other people I remember, your church would have a whole new set of problems. You'd be telling your pastor, "the church is getting too big, and we have too much money. What are we supposed to do?" Most pastors would love to have problems like that.

In almost every major world religion you find a few people who are set apart for some kind of important duty, a holy task, or some kind of religious leadership. Just about every religion has some kind of priest, monk, shaman, or whatever else the title may be. These are the "Holy People" set apart for specialized ministry and important duties.

In Christianity, what's the most important duty? Love the Lord thy God with all your heart, all your soul, all your mind, all your strength. The second major duty is to love your neighbor as you love yourself. This is the important stuff. This is the heart of our faith.

And there are other duties: love the sinner, feed the hungry, care for the sick, teach the children, forgive those who hurt you. This is the important "stuff". Whose job is it to do these things? These are everyone's job.

Teach people the truth, spread the gospel, and make disciples. Who should do these jobs? It's not just up to the pastors or priests. These are the duties of every believer.

One of the words that often gets mistranslated or misused in English is the word "Minister". What does minister mean? It does not mean "Holy Man" or priest. Minister is a verb. To minister to others means to serve or care for others. A minister is someone who sees to the need of someone else. And isn't that also everyone's job?

In the first century AD Christianity was often persecuted. Christians were accused of all sorts of vile things. How did things change? One thing that happened is Christians went that extra step to care for others. In those days it was quite common for a disease, such as the plague, to break out and consume a town. When that happened the healthy often escaped, leaving the sick behind. Christians would often stay and risk their lives to help others. Things like this showed the world Christians were not the monsters people said they were.

Centuries later Martin Luther and others began the reformation with three ideas in mind: 1. God saves us by giving us Jesus. 2. It is our faith in Jesus that saves, not our own works. 3. We are all priests. Martin Luther placed a great deal of emphasis on teachings like 1 Peter.

Peter was a disciple of Jesus. He was one of the "Big Guns" in the early church. He was the man who walked on water next to Jesus, the first to proclaim Jesus was the Messiah, the one Jesus said would be the cornerstone for the faith. It is Peter who tells us that all those who believe in Jesus are a **nation**. We are all one people bound together by our one leader. When we believe we are blessed, we are chosen, and we are **all** set apart for holy work. We are all priests in the eyes of God. Preaching sermons, baptizing a baby and serving communion is **not** more important than feeding the hungry, teaching the children and helping someone in need. All of these things are holy duties and we are all called on to do them.

So why do you have pastors? According to my seminary training the pastor's main job is to help everyone find their place; help everyone find their gifts and their ministry. Shall we feed the hungry and help the poor? Pastors can help with that but they can't do that alone. Who should preach sermons? Should the pastor be the only one? Who should go out, find the un-churched people, and teach them about our faith? It cannot fall on one person alone. How many doors are there to knock on in this area alone? How many more doors are there beyond this area? It would take a long time for one person to knock on them all.

To literally knock on doors intimidates some people, but do you know a few people who don't attend any church? What if everyone who attends this church were to invite just one person a month? And what if just 1 in 10 of the people you invite keeps coming? You could potentially double attendance in a year. You don't need a seminary degree to do that.

There's a church in Michigan who sees part of their ministry is simply to help people. The people became aware someone in the neighborhood wanted to get married, but they had almost nothing. So the church members and pastor agreed they would do the service for free. The people put together a potluck dinner for their reception. Someone bought a few flowers. And someone found their wedding dress and made sure it fit the bride. Guess which church saw quite an increase in attendance.

This is ministry. This is showing the love of Christ to others. You don't need ordination to do these things. You don't need a special blessing because you already have a special blessing when you say yes to God. All who believe have a special blessing from the Lord. And by doing these things you can be a special blessing to others.

The Disciples asked Jesus who would be the greatest disciple. Jesus answered the real leader was the servant. The greatest is the one who gives the most. Who were some of the greatest leaders of all time? Who were some of the best presidents America has ever had? We remember the names of those who gave the most, not the ones who took the most. The greatest saints in Christian history are not necessarily the ones who worked the most impressive miracles, but the ones who loved the most, and did the most good for others.

So, what Holy duties are there for us? There is an organization in America called Love Inc. It's an organization that tries to see to the needs of the poor and people with special needs. One of the people who works for them is a man with the calculator that has all that annoying paper coming out of it. This is the guy who balances the books for Love Inc. This is part of his ministry. There was someone else who collected food and clothes. There was someone else who collected furniture. And there were many others. That was their ministry.

One of the things they've been engaging in lately a ministry to teenage mothers. For a lot of our younger generation dinner is something you buy through a window or throw into a microwave. Convenient, but it's full of calories, fat, salt, artificial ingredients, and despite what many believe it is not really cheap. It's cheaper to buy some potatoes and fry them yourself than buy them through a drive through, but a lot of young girls don't know how to do this. Love Inc. has a program that has older women showing these young girls how to cook, how to shop, how to do laundry, and other housekeeping. Is there anyone here that could probably show a teenager how to cook, clean, sew, or balance a checkbook? This is ministry.

Not everyone can stand on a pulpit and preach. Not everyone can go stand on the street corner and preach. Not everyone can begin a mission in a foreign country. In fact not everyone can balance the books for a church or teach others how to cook. But every one of us is a minister. Every one of us already has a special blessing and a special call from God to go and do real ministry for the world.

The early church began without pastors and priests. It began with 12 disciples who knew Jesus, and a small crowd of people, who listened, obeyed, and did their part. The church grew and grew rapidly. It became an amazing movement within a few years. Within 300 years it had conquered the Roman Empire. When everyone looks upon themselves as a part of the church, a part of God's family, a priest of God, and when everyone does their part, miracles can happen.

Let's be part of God's plan to make some miracles, do God's holy work.

-In Jesus' name.

Advent Season: Add A Vent

Luke 11:24-25

Advent is the first season of the Christian calendar. It's the season we start over again and celebrate the year in a variety of ways: Advent, Christmas, Epiphany, Lent, and so on. So you might say last week began the Church New Year.

There is a great deal of uncertainty as to when the church started to recognize Advent as a special time of year but there is record of Advent taking place in 480 AD.

Advent is a time of preparation; time to make ready for Christmas. Today we celebrate Advent with scripture, special services, advent calendars, the advent wreath, and of course decorating. But over the centuries there have been other things associated with Advent.

In the past there were churches that encouraged fasting. It was known as the Nativity Fast or the Fast of December. Some Orthodox churches still observe it. A time of fasting, prayer and repentance are to discipline the body and our passions and focus on Godly things, not the physical, and draw closer to Christ.

Most of the readings and teachings during Advent focus on preparing for the birth of Jesus. But there is also supposed to be some focus on preparing for the second coming of Jesus. We had one Christmas and one day there will be another. Christ came, Christ died, Christ arose, and Christ will come again.

John the Baptist plays an essential role in the story of the first coming of Christ. According to the Luke narrative the

miraculous pregnancy of Martha preceded the miraculous pregnancy of Mary. John's birth foreshadowed Jesus' birth.
Years later it was the ministry of John that helped make the people ready for the ministry of Jesus. In fact many scholars think Jesus may have been a follower of John for a while. Perhaps he needed a little warm up himself.

But John's ministry was to proclaim the first coming of Jesus. He was called to prepare the way through repentance and purification. A new day was coming. A new act of God was at hand. John told the people to get ready for it and the best way to be ready was to repent, turn aside from sin, and turn back to God.

We often think of lent as a time to get rid of sin and that is true. But it's not a bad idea to clean house before Christmas either. The Christ child is coming into the world. Let's make ready by cleaning house and preparing our souls for the coming of the Lord.

In Latin the word is Adventus; meaning arrival or approach. In English it has much the same meaning. But, especially to the ears of a young children, sometimes one word might sound like another. So there have been jokes about how Advent is to "add a vent". Is that accurate? Of course not. But sometimes a silly play on words can have a meaning we never thought of.

What is a vent? A vent is some type of hole or opening that lets gas move around. When it gets pretty hot at home you might go upstairs to open a window to let hot air out. Or if you're in a room full of some smoke or a bad smell you might open a door or window to clean the air. That is venting.

Isn't that what John the Baptist was telling people to do; clean something out? His calling was to look at the sins of the people and call on them to clean house. "Look at your lives. Look at your words, your actions and the condition of your heart. Do you find some sin? Do you find something opposed to God? Then clean it out. It's time to air out a stinky house; clean out the sin. Clean out the things that drive you to evil and impurity. Clean out the things that hold you back from God." In a sense John is telling people, "add a vent to your souls."

Sins get in our way. Sins hold us back from God. When we are so focused on something ungodly then we become ungodly.

We've probably all heard about the 7 deadly sins, haven't we? We may not recall them perfectly but they are: Pride, Greed, Lust, Envy, Wrath, Sloth and Gluttony.

Pride. Many great theologians felt the heart of all sin was Pride. Pride is when you decide to set yourself in the middle of the universe; when we dare to believe it's all about me. And pride is especially when people are too ready to hold themselves above others; when they think they are better than others. Pride is destructive. It gives us a false sense of worth. It causes us to look down on others instead of loving them.

Greed: Greed keeps us focused on the wrong things. Usually earthly things. We want more and more instead of being happy with what we have. Greed consumes our heart.

Lust: We focus on the flesh; we focus on worldly pleasures instead of God. Pleasure becomes all consuming.

Envy: Kind of like greed. We see what others have and we want it. We want it so much it takes over our mind. It leads us to seeking the wrong things.

Wrath: Wrath can be terrible. Anger happens and anger can actually be a good thing. Anger can drive us to fight evil. But when anger becomes extreme, or turns to hate, it is nothing but destructive. People who hate try to harm others which can lead to the innocent being hurt and hateful people often destroy themselves.

Sloth: A little relaxation is necessary. Too much causes laziness, and laziness doesn't plant your crops or pay the bills.

Gluttony is also about worldly pleasure. Enjoying your food is good. Enjoying too much can also take over your mind and it can wreck your health.

These seven sins are different in some ways but they all have something in common; they distract our hearts and minds from things far more important. They consume us with things that are unhealthy for us spiritually, and mentally and even physically. When your mind is so possessed by lust, greed, envy, wrath, it doesn't just harm your soul, it can pollute your mind, interfering in your daily life. And aside from gluttony, the stress that can come from wrath, envy, greed can cause physical problems as well. Sin is unhealthy in so many ways.

John called on people to add a vent into their own lives. Prepare for the coming of the Messiah by letting the sin out.

But a vent can also be used to let something in. If we open 1 upstairs window to let hot air out, and a lower floor window to let cool air in, the house cools off a lot faster. When you open 2 windows, one to let the smells out and the other to let clean air in, the house cleans out faster.

Tis the season to Vent. Vent some sins out and vent in God.

Jesus once said,"*When the unclean spirit has gone out of a man, he roams through waterless places in search of rest; and finding none, he says, "I will return to my house which I left." And when he has come to it, he finds the place swept and clean. Then he goes and takes seven other spirits more evil than himself, and they enter in and dwell there; and the last state of that man becomes worse that the first* (Lk 11:24-25)."

When we drive a demon out of our lives, drive away some kind of sinful habits or something that pollutes us, that's great. It's great to clean out the house. But now the house is empty and empty things want to be filled. If no buys a house for a while and it sits vacant, sooner or later someone might notice and decide to occupy the house whether it's legal to or not. It happens fairly often in America. If we chase away sin but don't replace it with something it may come back.

Instead of just being empty of sin, lets fill that house with God.

Now is a great time to be filled with God because the evidence of God is all around us this time of year.

Although some of our decorations can be a bit secular, even pagan, although things can be too commercialized, too gaudy, they are set out to remind us of Christmas. They are there to remind us a great day is coming. God's day is coming. The word Christmas is from 2 old English words, Cristes maesse, which literally means "Christ's Mass". Christmas is about Jesus coming into the world.

And that is not just in the past. Advent has also been used as a time to remember that Christ will come again. Advent means every day is a good day to get ready for the second coming. It may not happen in our lifetimes but we should be ready for it. Who knows? Things do come unexpectedly.

Let's get ready for Christmas by adding 2 vents to our lives. Let's get some sin out and let lots of God in. Let's enjoy the season by rejoicing in our lights and ornaments but also by rejoicing in a new life. Christ has come and Christ makes a joyous new life. Christ brings the gift of new life and forgiveness. Let us rejoice in Christ our Lord.

Christmas Eve: Light in the Darkness

Luke 2:8-20

As you go forth from here today, take a moment to look up. What will you see? Stars. Centuries ago, people marveled at the stars because they didn't know what they were. Today, we know what they are. Scientist tell us they are giant fusion reactors. Gravity pulls hydrogen atoms together until they fuse together making helium, causing them to give off huge amounts of light and power. Knowing that makes them a little less mysterious I suppose. They seem less magical but there are still reasons to marvel.

Have you ever stopped to think about light? The stars are so far away from us that we don't even measure the distance in miles. We measure the distance in light years. It takes over two years for light from the closest stars to reach earth. Some of the stars we see with our naked eyes are hundreds, maybe thousands of light years away. When we look at the stars, we are looking at light that probably began its journey before Columbus crossed the ocean or maybe even before Jesus was born. When you look at a star you are really looking back in time.

Thanks to modern technology, we have super telescopes that can see the light of stars that are even further away. Even though our naked eyes can't see it there is light in our night sky that has been traveling for billions of years. Imagine, light that is so dim our eyes can't see it. Even Trillions of miles of darkness and billions of years of time cannot truly consume the light of the stars.

The Bible says about 2000 years ago, another kind of light was born here on earth. It came to us in a small stable, in a tiny town, in a little baby. He came to bring light to the world. He came to show us the true nature of God. He came to make a change in the world itself.

Yet many never saw him. All they saw was darkness. They were too blinded by the world around them to see the wondrous light that was Jesus.

But some saw and some believed. They saw the light that came into the world and how the darkness tried to hide it. The darkness tried to consume him. But darkness cannot overcome light.

Over the centuries many others have tried to eliminate this light. Dictators, empires, nations, philosophers, scientists, great thinkers, and so many others, have tried to exterminate the light of Jesus. And they all have one thing in common, they've all failed.

Yes, there have been times when the light was hard to see. There have been days when it seems like the darkness won. But we are here tonight because that light has not gone out and we are the proof. The light of Jesus shines on in our hearts, and so it shines on in our world.

Some may have forgotten the true nature of the light. Christmas has become just a holiday for some people, its true meaning forgotten. But there is light in the message and there is still light in us. As long as we remember and as long as we believe, the light of God's own son will not be forgotten.

And it's up to us to spread the good news of this light. One night, a bright light appeared to some shepherds and an angel told them a baby was born who would be the savior. They listened, they went, they saw, and they believed. And then the shepherds went forth to spread this wondrous good news. Even though these people lived in great darkness- they lived under the harsh boot of the Roman Empire, God had not forgotten them. God came to show them that a new light was born.

The dark times will come. People have this tendency to bring evil to the world. Dictators will rise and oppression may last for a while, but God is always God and God does not forget us. God is with us even today. God sent us a great light 2000 years ago and that light is still bright today. The darkness has not overcome it and never will.

So let us rejoice tonight in the light of God's love and go forth to spread this good news once again.

Behold, I bring you good news of great joy that shall be for all the people. For unto you, all of you, all over the world, the savior is born. He is Christ the Lord. God has not forgotten us. God has sent a great light unlike any ever seen before. God is here. God is with us. God's light shines in our world tonight.

Rejoice in the Lord this joyous Christmas night. Give glory to God in the highest and give glory to God here on earth. And on earth let there be peace and goodwill to all people, everywhere.

In Jesus' name.

Good Friday: The Ultimate Transfusion

Luke 23:26-46; John 19:17-30

As a child I often found it confusing that we would call the Friday before Easter "Good Friday." Jesus was crucified, murdered in a horrible way, died and was buried. That didn't sound like something good to me and I know many other people agree with that. I've been told some people actually do call it, "Bad Friday" or "dark Friday." We know some people called it, "God's Friday," and it's possible that title morphed into "Good Friday."

But if we are going to call it Good Friday what makes it so good?

Most Christians agree Good Friday was the day Jesus sacrificed himself for the good of the world. Jesus gave his life to save us all from our sins. So it is a good Friday for humanity, but how does dying bring salvation?

The most common view today seems to be that God is a God of love, but God is also a God of justice. People sin and sin leads to death. Since all have sinned and fall short of the glory of God then all people are removed from God and deserving of death. In order to be saved from sin there must be atonement.

The Old Testament talks about the many sins that must be atoned for and offers many details about how to sacrifice animals in payment for sin. By the blood of the animals the debts are paid, and the sins are forgiven.

So most Christians teach Jesus came and he paid the price one time and for all people. He didn't offer up the blood of animals to pay for sin. He offered his own life and died to be the one great sacrifice for all people and forever.

That is probably the most common view today but it's not the only one. Over the centuries there have been theologians who looked at the sacrifice of Jesus in different ways.

There's a sermon I sometimes preach in September about Yom Kippur. Yom Kippur is the Jewish New Year. It's also called the Day of Atonement. It's a holiday that goes clear back to the days of Moses. Leviticus 16 calls on all the people of Israel to have a day to atone for the sins of all the people. On that day two goats were brought to the temple for sacrifice.

One was the scapegoat. A red ribbon was tied into the horns of the goat, prayers were said over the goat, and it was sent out into the wilderness to carry away the sins of the people.

The other goat was a blood sacrifice. This goat was taken to the temple, prayed over, then it was killed, and the blood was poured onto the altar in the temple. This represented the sins of all the people being washed away or covered up by the blood of the goat.

This can be confusing for some people because we are left to wonder which is it? Does the scapegoat take away the sins of the people? Or does the blood of the other goat wash away the sins? Or does the blood of the goat paint over sins of the people as some teach? This seems somewhat contradictory and confusing.

So when Jesus died on the cross what was he? Was he a sacrifice because God demands a death to atone for all sins? Was he a scapegoat who takes all our sins with him into tomb and buries them forever? Or was he the sacrificial goat who washed away the sins of the world?

It may be confusing to us but not to the people in the ancient world. The bible tells us women went to the tomb to anoint Jesus' body the Sunday after he died. What happened when they got to the tomb? One gospel says there was one angel there and he rolled aside the stone. But in another gospel, it says the stone was already rolled away and there were two angels in the tomb. Isn't this a contradiction? Not to them. In Jewish thought the one angel represented one truth. The two angels represented another truth. For them it is not a contradiction.

So was Jesus a payment to God for sin? A scapegoat? A cleansing sacrifices? Or a covering for sin? In Jewish thought he could be all four at the same time. The end result is somehow Jesus buys salvation with his own life.

But if God is so loving why would he do this? Why would God make his Son die on a cross? In the books of the prophets we often see God telling the people if they will simply repent and return to their faith God would forgive them. The Bible tells us King David sinned a great sin. The prophet Samuel confronted him and showed him his fault. But Samuel told him he was forgiven (2 Samuel 12:13). The Bible doesn't say anything about David offering a sacrifice or some other ritual. He was already forgiven.

If David and others can simply be forgiven, then was the cross necessary? Did Jesus really need to die? Some people will obviously say absolutely yes. Some will never believe there could be an alternative. But some people will say 'perhaps there was another way.' What is the truth?

The truth is actually kind of obvious when you think about it. If there was another way what does that mean? It means Jesus chose to die; Jesus CHOSE the cross. Think about what that means for a moment. If Jesus had options, then he chose the most painful and humiliating one of them all.

Why would he choose that one? Maybe it's because we NEEDED to see how extreme our sins are. He needed to show us how horrific sins and can. He showed us how painful it is to God when we sin and wander from him. In other words God does not need the blood. We need the blood. The blood is not for the sake of some bloodthirsty monster in heaven. It is for our sake that Jesus died. Just as we might give our blood to save another so Jesus gave his blood to save us all. Blood is life. So Jesus gave us his life.

And the cross also means that we needed to see the great example of how great is God's love for us. Just as a mother would sacrifice herself for the sake of her children, so God makes a great sacrifice for the sake of all God's children.

And that's not the best part of the story. The loving generosity of this sacrifice will soon give way to the incomparable wonder of the Resurrection. God's love will be revealed like never before, because even death will not hold back the love and the amazing power of our God. Jesus is risen to show that our salvation is complete, that our place is with God, and that nothing, not even death, will defeat God's will for us. This is the beauty that the blood of Christ has brought to us. This is the majesty of the day of Resurrection.

Thanks be to Christ our Lord. Amen.

Easter Sunday: An Empty Tomb

1 John 1:1-10; Luke 24: 1-12

"Who Moved the Stone?" That's the name of a book first written in 1930 by a man named Frank Morison.

He was a lawyer and a skeptic in regard to Jesus. He set out to find proof the Resurrection of Jesus never happened. He did his research, studied, and in the end, he concluded the stone was moved by an act of God because Jesus really did rise from the dead. He set out to refute the Resurrection and found himself converted by the evidence.

I have heard many times that there are lawyers who say they could win over a 12-person jury with the evidence that Jesus rose. Many others have come to look at the evidence and found themselves walking away believers.

Skeptics of course aren't so ready to jump on the believer band wagon. If you've studied history, especially ancient religions, you learn stories of other people or gods who have supposedly died and then been raised from the dead.

If you've read the book "The World's 16 Crucified Saviors" you know some people try to equate the Resurrection of Jesus with other characters. If you've seen the movie "Religulous" you might have seen there are some of the similarities between Jesus and the Egyptian god Horus. It can challenge your faith, until you do what I did; I read real Egyptian history. Most of the so-called similarities between Jesus and Horus are complete fiction. This movie and the book misrepresent the truth and rely very heavily on inaccuracies or even outright lies.

If you're interested, it was Horus' father, Osirus, that was supposedly killed and raised from the dead. Isis raised Osirus from the dead long enough to conceive and eventually give birth to Horus, so he was not born of a virgin. There is no reason to believe he was born in December (even if he was that is a pointless argument since Jesus probably wasn't born in December either. Horus he did not have followers, he was not known as a healer or savior and there are many other false allegations and discrepancies. Supposedly Horus did rise from the dead and he still rises to this very day; he rises every day with the rising sun. There's a big difference between that and a Resurrection.

As for Osiris being raised, it is simply a story. There are no witnesses or other evidence, but there were witnesses to Jesus risen from the dead. Whoever wrote the story of Horus was probably just copying one old story after another and embellishing.

The same is true of most other so called "Resurrection stories." Most were written centuries after the supposed event. Most were never witnessed by anyone. And as to the ones that were supposedly witnessed, quite often the so-called witnesses were ordered or threatened to "witness" the event. That is history. That is reality.

In the Bible things are different.

From the letter of first John 1, "That which was from the beginning, which we have heard, which we have seen with our eyes, which we have looked at **and our hands have touched."** The first few words are amazing in themselves. "That which was from the beginning." He is saying Jesus was more than a man. He believed and taught that somehow Jesus existed before the creation of the world itself. That is an amazing thing for a man of Jewish background to state because they teach only God existed in the beginning. It would be blasphemous to say otherwise. But John said it.

Then John said something that is almost as amazing, "That which we have heard, which we have seen with our eyes, which we have looked at **and our hands have touched**." Heard. Seen. Touched. John is literally saying this is not some old legend that someone else supposedly saw. John saw it with his own eyes. "And our hands have touched." He claims he physically touched Jesus after he was supposedly dead. This was not a ghost. This was not a vision. This was not a dream. This was real.

And in his gospel John states very clearly there were others who saw it as well. The Bible tells us there were 12 disciples. One became a traitor and died, so there were 11 disciples who saw this. And there were others who saw it, like Mary Magdalene. Each one of the 11 disciples went to their grave saying it was true. Tradition says John is the only one who lived to an old age and died a natural death. All the others were killed, murdered or executed rather than say it wasn't true. John is trying to be as clear as possible: "This was real and we are witnesses."

Most experts believe the writings of John were made before 100 AD. That would be less than 70 years after the Resurrection.

The other gospels and New Testament writings were not written in the second century as some people claim. There is ample evidence that at least one gospel was written before 70 AD, about 40 years after the Resurrection. And there evidence that at least parts of the gospels were written before that. Many of Paul's writings were written before 60 AD.

And many of the NT writings were based on the testimony of witnesses, not old legends.

There are actual fragments of the New Testament that have been dated to the early second century and they did not just appear out of nowhere. They were based on other writings that must have been written before the year 100.

Obviously, 2000 years later, we have no photos, no videos, no fingerprints. We do not have absolute proof it happened. Skeptics will always say what they say and they make good arguments. Skeptics are often and they know what they are doing. No matter what evidence we may find today it will never be perfect. There will always be some faith required. But our faith should not be called "blind faith." We have logical and real reasons to believe what we believe.

John would also write, "the life appeared; we have seen it and testify to it…"

The Resurrection was real, but since it took place nearly 2000 years ago what could it mean to us today? How can it be relevant?

Well, people invented farming, and even selective breeding of plants and animals, thousands of years ago. Where would we be today without them?

The Egyptians forged metal and made glass more than 1000 years before Jesus was born. Don't those things matter to us today?

The Greeks came up with complex math decades before Jesus was born; math that is used everyday.

Edward Jenner invented a vaccine for smallpox in 1796. Louis Pasteur invented a vaccine for rabies in the 1880s. The principles they used to make those vaccines then are the same principles we use today.

The past is always with us. Even the ancient past matters in a modern world.

Jesus' Resurrection is not "old news." It's not something that only mattered 2000 years ago. It matters today.

I often ask people questions like, "Does aspirin cure a headache?" The answer is actually **NO**. Aspirin doesn't do a thing for us if we leave it in the bottle. The Bible has certainly had a major influence on our modern world. It does matter in our world and in our daily lives. But it might not mean much in our personal lives if Jesus is in a book on the shelf that we never touch. Even the risen Jesus doesn't do much for us if we ignore him.

But when we make him part of our lives amazing things can happen.

I was raised in a household where we often went to church. As a child I hated going to church. When I started college I began in Data Processing; not ministry.

As a teen I was often depressed, not happy, and had a rather negative view on life and myself.

But at age 18, before I started college, I gave my life to Jesus. And my friends will tell you, I changed a lot as a person and in my outlook on life. My sisters have often joked about the brother they had to drag into church and how "He became a pastor???" God works in mysterious ways. God made a change in my life because of an empty tomb.

An empty tomb means death is overcome. An empty tomb means a change in the world. An empty tomb means salvation. Sin is conquered.

And an empty tomb can change lives. My life changed. Many lives have been changed because of an empty tomb.

Jesus came to change lives and by so doing change the world.

Jesus died and rose again around 30 A.D. For about 300 years after that Christians were persecuted in many parts of the Roman empire. People were even crucified for being Christians. But during those 300 years of stress and persecution, more and more people gave their lives to Christ, even though it could have meant death.

And around 300 AD, a new Emperor came to power and made Christianity legal. Jesus conquered an empire without sword and shield but by the power of his truth and love. An empty tomb defeated the power of the Caesars.

In the early 20th century a great threat came to the world in the form of Russian communism. For about 70 years the world lived under a very dark cloud, especially when nuclear weapons came along.

Then, a mere 70 years later, the Berlin wall came down. One reason it crumbled is because of the great faith of the Polish people. They dedicated their lives to God, to Jesus, and to peacefully resisting evil. One of the greatest threats to life on earth died because of an empty tomb.

Is there tension in the world today? Is there great worry? Yes there is. But Jesus can and will prevail again especially if we hold to the faith.

That is the power of faith. Jesus came to this world to live in our lives, in our hearts, and be part of us.

When we talk about God and salvation quite a few people think about the afterlife. People think about what will happen when we die. Yes, that is part of our faith but only one part. The tomb is not empty just so we can get to heaven. Salvation is about the here and now. Salvation is about changing our lives today so that we become a new creation, a better people.

Jesus came to transform us. A type of Resurrection can take place in us when we let Jesus into our lives. There are many parts of us that we never even think about. Things we may be unaware of. When we give our lives to Christ there are parts of us, we never even knew we had that can spring to life.

We get to have a new life in Jesus. We get to rise above what we were and be more like the people God wants us to be.

An empty tomb brings a full life to Jesus and to us.

Today is a great day to reach out and grab that new life. Today is a great day to pray and say "Jesus, come into my life. Make me a new creation. May your Resurrection live in me now in this life and forever. "

In Jesus name.

World Communion Sunday: The Story of Bread

Exodus 12:39; John 6:48-59

Bread: How many of us have some kind of bread product on our shopping list just about every week? Bread, biscuits, muffins, cake. You may not think of cookies, spaghetti, pasta or crackers as bread, but they are in the same general category.

Where did it all start?

Archeologists have found evidence people started collecting and boiling grains thousands of years ago. Our ancestors ate things akin to gruel or mush long ago. But it's still a bit of a jump from soggy grains to bread. What happened?

One theory is that some naughty little boy didn't want to finish his mush (children have always been children) so he hid his bowl of warm, soggy grain. And then maybe something as simple as a gentle breeze blew yeast or some other bacteria into the bowl. Hours later someone found the bowl and discovered that it had puffed up. That may have been the big step that would eventually lead to making bread.

In almost every corner of the world people eat something rich in starches and almost all of those people have found a way to turn their starches into some kind of bread.

Asian countries rely on plain rice but they also make noodles, which is where pasta comes from. And many make some type of rice bread. (It is quite sticky.)

When Europeans came to North America, they found the natives raised sweet corn but they also had the colorful "Indian

Corn" that we decorate with in the fall. You don't boil it and chew it like sweet corn but you can crush it into a flour and make a type of bread.

In the old seafaring days sailors did not exactly travel with a lot of bread but they had ship biscuits, or hard tack, which is flour cooked into a little cake and is hard as a rock. And of course sailors needed something to drink and it could be hard to keep fresh water clean. So most European ships had a beer that was low in alcohol for their sailors. In fact beer has been known as "liquid bread" by some people.

So bread is almost a universal food. And we tend to take it for granted. We don't always appreciate just how important bread has been in history and its importance in life.

Bread has changed cultures. If you can't grow one type of grain you better grow another, and your society has to adjust to the type of grains you grow. Some types of grain can be fairly easy to grow so you don't need a lot of farmers. But others are difficult to grow, so farming becomes everyone's job. And if you need large tracts of land to grow your grains, but you don't have much, then you might go to war with your neighbor. Societies have changed because of bread.

Bread is made from grains that are usually available in abundance or easy to grow in large quantities. It would take a lot of land to grow enough fruits and vegetables to feed large populations but you can grow lots of grain on that land to make into bread. Bread often fills you up better than fruits and vegetables. Bread, made from whole grains, is high in fiber and other nutrients. And bread contains the carbohydrates that help keep your body fueled.

The old joke about putting someone in jail and feeding them only "bread and water" isn't just a joke. You can survive on a diet of just bread at least for a while.

When the Russians invaded Afghanistan in the 70s the Afghans fought back. They often traveled by foot or on horseback. They climbed some pretty tall mountains and fought hard on a diet consisting largely of bread and tea.

So when Jesus said things like "I am the bread of life," think for a minute about what that really means.

One day Jesus has a crowd of 5000 people and he wants to feed them. A little boy offered Jesus his lunch. His mother probably filled a sack with 2 fish, probably not much bigger than sardines, and 5 small loaves of what looked like Pita bread, each one probably the size of a small pancake. That was his sack lunch.

If you sat down for a meal in Nazareth around 30 AD what would be on the menu? Maybe a few fruits or vegetables like olives, figs, some greens. Maybe you'd enjoy some milk or cheese. Once in a while some lamb or goat but that would be a rare treat for the average family.

In the center of your plate would be bread. For thousands of years, in most of the societies of the world, some kind of bread was literally the center of your meal.

So when Jesus says, "I am the bread of life" he is not saying "I'm a taste of your favorite food" or "an important food." Jesus is saying, "I am the center of your plate. I am the heart and soul of every meal you have ever eaten in your life."

Or perhaps Jesus is trying to say, "I should be the center of your plate. I want to be the center of your plate. Bread is life, and I want to be the heart and soul of your life." That is Jesus.

Jesus brings us God's word, and God's word is supposed to be the center of our lives.

The Bible says we are made in God's image. Just as our bodies don't function well without bread how can our lives function properly without God? How can we be the people of God if we don't open our hearts and let God in?

There are many diets for weight loss in the world. In at least one of them you don't focus on calories, you focus on the nutrients. If you find yourself eating white bread and still feel hungry it's because white bread has been stripped of the nutrients your body needs. But if you eat a couple pitas or some whole grain corn bread it can be very filling because it has the nutrients the body needs.

Jesus is nutrition. Jesus fills us with what we **NEED**. Jesus teaches us we are part of something far greater than we can imagine. Jesus brings a message of hope, a message of love, a message of forgiving and a message of healing. That is what we need. That is God's word. It fills us, nourishes us, and helps us to be the people we are meant to be because it feeds the image of God in us.

And it gives us fuel we need to get face life and its struggles.

After funerals I often try to spend some time with the family. It's hard to remember how many times someone has told me they couldn't have gotten through it without their faith.

The early church and many Christians across the centuries have had to endure hardship and persecution. What kept them going? It was the belief that Jesus was with them. They felt their message was needed to save the world even though the world was against them. Jesus gave them the strength and endurance that comes from faith, hope, and love.

Jesus is the universal food that all people need.

What kind of bread would you like? We have white, wheat, rye, barley, corn, quinoa, potato, oat, multigrain and pumpernickel. Or do you prefer Italian, French, sweet bread, sourdough, beer bread, pita, rice or flat bread? Maybe some biscuits, pasta, Pumpkin bread, zucchini bread, raisin bread or carrot cake? And there's more.

There are many different types of bread in the world, but they are all so similar in so many ways. Take some starchy grain, preferably high in fiber, mix it with water and other ingredients, then cook it. Many types of bread but they all do the same thing. They fill you up, fuel your body and keep you going.

We are different but communion is one of those things that shows us we are not too different. In so many ways we are the same.

Just like bread people come an amazing variety; white and black and brown and Asian, male and female, tall and short, young and old. But we are all human beings. We may look different but there is only 1 race, the human race. All people need bread. All people need God. All people need Jesus. All people need God's word.

So all kinds of people are welcome, especially on this special day. During a 24-hour period, millions of people, different kinds of people, from all over the world will break bread and drink from a cup. It may not be the same kind of bread, it may not be the same kind of drink, but it all represents one Jesus, the universal bread and universal savior.

Today we are part of a greater whole. Today we are all people of God, filled with God, being fed by the one true God.

So let us gather around God's table. This is a gift of God given for you. This is a meal of joy and celebration because it means we are all part of each other. This meal is a hint of who Jesus was and what he did for us. Let us make Jesus the center of our plates, the center of our lives, and the bread of our souls.

In Jesus' name.

Yom Kippur: The Two Goats

Leviticus 16: 7-8, 15-22

In 1970 a very fascinating organization was formed, "Jews for Jesus." This organization is made up largely of Jewish people who do believe and proclaim that Jesus really was the Messiah that people have been seeking for centuries.

To prove their point they go through the scriptures to find proof of who and what Jesus was. One of their greatest arguments comes from Leviticus 16.

Each September our Jewish brethren will be celebrating Rosh Hashanah, The Jewish New Year. It's one of the greatest celebration days on the Jewish calendar.

And then they will celebrate the service of Yom Kippur. About 1300 years before the birth of Christ God appeared to Moses and gave him instructions for what is called, "The Day of Atonement;" Yom Kippur.

First there are 9 days of repentance and fasting. A time for the people to look into themselves, examine their own lives, face their sins, and turn from them. Then the day of Atonement begins.

First the High Priest was required to sacrifice a bull for his own sins. Only after this was he considered cleansed of sin and "Pure Enough" to enter the Holy of Holies in the temple.

After this came the time to choose two goats by lot. Although Yom Kippur is especially a time for personal repentance, it was also a time when the priests were to offer a sacrifice for all the people of Israel for all their sins.

The first goat was led to the altar in the temple. Prayers were made, the goat was sacrificed, and the blood was poured onto the altar. The blood represented cleansing the people of their sins.

The second goat had a different job. This is where the word scapegoat comes from. This goat was taken by the priests, and a red cord was tied around its horns. The priests would then pray over the goat, laying all the sins of all the people upon the goat. The goat would then be taken outside of town, given a kick and sent out into the wilderness. In this way all the sins of all the people are laid on the goat and the goat would carry the sins away.

What would happen to the scapegoat? Obviously some of them would die in the wilderness. But quite a few would live, at least for a while, and sometimes someone would see the goat and report what they had seen. It was very important to notice what happened to the ribbon. If the ribbon had remained red, then some believed the prayers were unanswered and the sins remained on the people.

But, sometimes, people would see the goat, and report that the red cord had turned white. This was said to be a powerful sign; a sign that all the sins of all the people had been carried away and that God had redeemed his people. God forgave them.

This ritual was done every year because every year new sins were committed, the people had a time to repent again, and two new goats were taken to the temple for the Day of Atonement. This went on for centuries.

But around the year 70 AD, disaster came to Israel. The Romans were fed up with the troublesome people in Judea and they put Jerusalem under siege. Eventually the priests in the temple knew the end was coming, so they wrote out their memoirs. One thing they felt the need to record was that they had faithfully held to the traditions of Yom Kippur every year but something was wrong. They reported that for about 40 years no one had seen the red cord on the scapegoat turn white. For 40 years Israel was without this great sign.

Please remember, the people writing these memoirs were not Christians. These memoirs were written by priests in the temple who did not approve of Christianity. They are the ones who felt the need to record that for 40 years no one saw the ribbon turn white. It was as if the scapegoats were no longer effective. Or perhaps they were just no longer needed. Perhaps something, or maybe someone, had taken away the sins of the people starting around the year 30 AD.

When was Jesus crucified? Most scholars agree it was around the year 30 AD. Is that just a coincidence, or did something extraordinary happen? Sometimes the lack of a sign can be the biggest sign of all.

As we follow the Bible we see God is often bringing about something new. God frequently takes people, and even the nation, a new direction.

Abraham was born near the city of Ur in Mesopotamia and he may have been happy there. He might have been happy to spend the rest of his life in Ur. Or perhaps he would have eventually decided to wander but he could easily have chosen to go north, south or eat. It was all up to him. At least it was up to him until God stepped in and did something new. God called on him to move west and when he did God moved history a new direction.

When Jacob and his family moved into Egypt history took another turn.

Then when Moses led the people out of Egypt history really took a sharp turn.

In Jesus Christ history took an amazingly sharp turn. Animal sacrifice was common in many cultures in the ancient world. Today we no longer have them because Christianity is a change in religion itself. Religion is people searching for God. In Christ, God takes that and turns it completely on its head. Christ has come down to earth to lift us up because we cannot pull ourselves up to God.

In the story of the good shepherd, a man has 100 sheep. One gets lost. What does the shepherd do? Wait and say, "Oh well he'll show up sooner or later"? Does he just forget it and look after the other 99? No, the good shepherd is the one who goes and seeks the lost.

Jesus is God seeking the lost.

As we know there are many different ways of looking at some things in the Bible, but our faith teaches that when Jesus died on the cross, he cleansed all the sins of the world with his own blood. Jesus took the sins of the world onto himself. When he died, he carried our sins into the grave. And when he arose he left our sins behind. Jesus became our scapegoat.

People often say there are contradictions in the Bible. Are there? Take a look at story from Leviticus again. The first goat was sacrificed. Its blood was poured out onto the altar. Did it wash the sins away or does it cover the sins? Not everyone is n full agreement.

But then the second goat is sent out into the wilderness and supposedly carries the sins away. Why do we need to have the sins carried off if they are already washed away? Or painted over? Isn't that a contradiction?

Not if you understand the world as the Hebrew people did. For them there is no contradiction. All three can be correct at the same time in some way.

What do the scriptures tell us? Some verses in the New Testament say Jesus washed away our sins. But some say he carried away our sins. And some people believe they were buried in the tomb but when Jesus arose he rose above the sins and left them behind. In some hymns we sing about being washed in the blood. In other hymns, such as "It is Well," we sing how our sins are 'nailed to the cross and I bear them no more.' Which one is the truth?

Why do we have to settle for one? Can't Jesus pay the price, and cover over the sins, and wash them away, and carry them away all at the same time? In Jewish theology there is no contradiction; all of the above can be true at the same time.

Whatever your personal understanding may be, the heart of our faith is that Jesus takes away the sins of the world; we are cleansed, we are healed, we are forgiven because of Jesus.

Why do we need to settle on just one image of what that means? No two people will agree on everything. People often look at the same word or the same situation in different ways. People don't understand everything the same way. Perhaps the different theories of salvation are meant to mean different things to different people so we can all understand them in our own way. I can believe something different than you and still be a Christian because Jesus is the Christ of all no matter how we may understand the world. Jesus is savior of all because God is far more than anything we can imagine.

At one time we looked to bloody sacrifices as an avenue to God. Today we don't make an avenue to God, God makes an avenue to us. A new life, a new world, and a new kind of religion, was born when Christ became our scapegoat to take the sins of the world away. We no longer need goats and ribbons and blood on the altar. The greatest, most cleansing blood of all, was spilled on a cross for the salvation of the world.

We may never fully understand what that means but we know in Christ there is salvation because Christ has taken away the sins of the world.

In Jesus name.

The Greatest Commandment: Love

1 Corinthians 13; Matthew 22:34-40

"Love is a many splendored thing" – "My love is like a red, red rose." – "Love is composed of a single soul inhabiting two bodies." – "Love is a bridge bringing two people together." – "Love makes the world go around." – All this and so much more is love.

Someone once asked Jesus, "What is the greatest commandment." Jesus replied, "Hear of Israel, The Lord our God, The Lord is one. You shall love The Lord your God with all your heart with all your soul, with all your mind and with all your strength. And the second is like it; you shall love your neighbor as you love yourself."

Love is at the very heart of Christianity. "For God so loved the world that he gave his only Son." John 3:16. That alone tells us much about God. The reason Jesus came to the earth, the heart of our faith and salvation, is found in just a few words, "For God so loved the world."

In America Love is one of those words we toss around so often, and use it in so many different ways, that it becomes hard to define. Is love all about feelings? Is love about family and friends? Is love about really liking something? Or does love mean "all of the above and more?"

Around the world, no matter what the culture or beliefs, people have a word, or words, that indicate strong, positive, emotions: like kindness, compassion, affection or warmth. People have words that indicate a strong bond, like the bond between mother and child. People use words that indicate passion, devotion, intimacy. So in many ways people recognize love as more than one thing.

Love plays an important part in many world religions.

In Buddhism the word Karuna is compassion and mercy, which reduces the suffering of others. This is necessary for enlightenment. Adveṣa and mettay are benevolent love. This love is unconditional and implies unselfish interest in others' welfare.

Hinduism also believes in karuna, compassion and mercy, which impels one to help reduce the suffering of others. But the word Bhakti is a term meaning, "loving devotion to the supreme God."

In the Jewish and Christian beliefs, Love is and has always been a very central theme of our faith.

The first 5 books of the Bible, Genesis, Exodus, Leviticus, Numbers and Deuteronomy, are often called the books of Moses. More properly they are called the Torah. What does Torah mean? Many think it means law. Not exactly. The true translation is, "The love of God expressed through law." God sends us laws for our own good. One of the ways God's love is expressed is by sending us guidance.

In fact love might very well be the answer to some of our most profound questions. Why did God make the universe? Some people say God was lonely? That's unusual because some people would say loneliness is an imperfection. How can a perfect God contain an imperfection? Perhaps the real answer is that God is simply a creator and a creator needs to create something.

Or perhaps God is love and for love to be real we need someone or something to love. So perhaps the instant God thought of us, God loved us and decided to create us. If so then we were created to love and be loved by God. Perhaps the reason we exist is because creation is an act of love.

When Jesus speaks in Matthew 22 and says the greatest command is to "Love the Lord your God with all your heart, with all your soul, with all your mind, and with all your strength," he wasn't exactly original. That teaching was written in Deuteronomy hundreds of years before Jesus was born.

In fact, as you enter a Jewish home you might see a small scroll in a decorative case in the door. That is called a mezuzah. It contains scripture verses from Deuteronomy 6:4-9 and 11:13-21. The verses are used as a prayer called the Shema. It begins with the phrase: "Hear, O Israel, Jehovah (is) our God, Jehovah is One. You shall love the Lord your God with all your heart, with all your soul and with all you might." The scroll is there to take Deuteronomy 6:9 very literally, "write the words of God on the gates and doorposts of your house."

And Jesus' second teaching, "Love your neighbor as you love yourself," was also written in the Bible, Leviticus 19:18, long before he said them.

But again, what does it really mean?

The New Testament was originally written in Greek. There were at least 4 words in Greek that meant love. Two of those words, Eros and Storge, are not in the New Testament. Eros is about sexuality, as is in the word "erotic." Storge is about family love, like parent and child.

The two words that are in the New Testament are the words Philia and Agape.

Philia is about friendship but is often used to mean brotherly love. The word Philadelphia means "The City of Brotherly

Love." And there are many instances in the Bible where Jesus or a disciple talked about brotherly love.

But the word that appears most in the Bible is the word Agape. It was in use hundreds of years before Jesus' birth and it underwent some changes. It has been used many different ways but by the time of Jesus it was seen as a "Self-emptying or divine love."

Christians started to see it as "the highest form of love." It was used to describe the love that comes from God or Christ; the perfect love of God for man and of man for God.

And it is a kind of love that goes beyond the emotions. It's the love of that leads people to seek the best for others regardless of the circumstances. It is a universal, unconditional love.

Perhaps the best example is mother and child. We certainly want our children to turn out well. We want them to live good, happy, worthwhile lives. But some children go wrong. What happens when they do? We hope they straighten up. We hope we can help them to go right.

But imagine a child getting worse and worse. Imagine a child who grows up to be about as evil as a person can be. What would the mother think? Is she thinking, "I hate you and I will kill you," or is she thinking, "No matter how evil you are I will always hope you will change. I will always hope that somehow something good comes out of you. I will never want to see you suffer and die"?

That is how it should be for parent and child. And that is how it is for God and humanity.

Have you ever looked at the world, at your fellow human beings, and asked yourself, "How can God put up with us?" It's easy to see why someone would tell the story of Noah.

There is darkness in the human heart so deep that sometimes it's easy to think God should wipe us out and start over.

But God does not. God lets this world keep on turning. God lets the human race continue to be what it is and progress the way it does. Why? Because God loves us as we are; flaws and all.

That does not mean God always likes us. Christians and Jews and others believe in something called sin. There are many things we can do but God does not want us to do. There are behaviors, words, and even thoughts that God does not like. There are things in us that are anti-God and obviously God does not approve. But does God's dislike and disapproval end God's love for us?

How many of us have children who have never once broken a rule? Do you like absolutely everything about your children, or do they have at least a few habits, activities, or personality traits you really dislike? Do your children have friends you don't like? Or did your child marry someone you don't like? You probably don't always like your own child, but do you ever stop loving them? For a parent there will always be a positive feeling. You will always remember that day when you first held them in your arms. That memory and that emotional bond will never go away.

So it is with God. God has a powerful emotional bond for us that will never go away.

But what is it like for us? We are not God. What happens when someone does something horrible? What about when the deepest evil possible comes out of us? How are we supposed to love one another when someone goes way too far?

Polly Klaas was a child when she was murdered by Richard Allen Davis. During his trial Richard Allen Davis was anything but remorseful. I once wrote a letter to Marc Klaas, the father, and I expressed my sympathy. But I also told him, "Richard Allen Davis started life like all of us. Once he was an innocent baby himself. Why did he go so wrong? Perhaps remembering that we all started the same can help us love one another." It is possible for us to feel something, even for a monster.

The other truth to remember is love is not just an emotion. Remember the word Agape; love that goes beyond the emotions. Love of that leads people to seek the best for others regardless of the circumstances.

In the Bible love is not just about our feelings. Love is also something we do. One definition for biblical love is giving of yourself to someone else. Or choosing to give of yourself to another.

After World War 2 ended, there's a story of a woman who reached through the barbed wire and held out her hand to one of the guards. Did she like everything about him? No. Did she like everything he did? Obviously not. But she made a choice. She chose to care even for such a man.

Some years ago, a young Korean man was visiting America. He was murdered and his killers were brought to court. His parents wrote the court asking for a lenient sentence for the killers and promising to help them if they could when they got out. They chose to reach out. They chose to care.

Romantic love is a gift from God. Family and friendship love are gifts from God. And there is a love far beyond the ordinary and it is a gift from God. We can choose to care no matter what. We can choose to give of ourselves. It's not always easy, and it's not always painless, but it is a profound and deep love that benefits you and benefits the world. And it is the ultimate love that God calls on us to do; not feel but do.

Love is a verb. Love is an action. And this kind of love is the most splendid thing of all.

May this kind of love live in you that you may carry this love into all the world.

In Jesus' name.

God Always Does the Wrong Thing

Jeremiah 28:1-9, John 2:13-22, 1 Corinthians 1:18-25

Did you ever notice God does the wrong thing? That sounds like a silly thing to say, and perhaps even blasphemous, but there is a lot of truth in that statement.

Looking back about 4000 years we see the story of Abraham. Abraham was a righteous man but he had a problem; he needed a son and heir to his property. During their encounters God promised Abraham he would have a son but the child didn't come very quickly. So Abraham did what people do; he took matters into his own hands. He had a child with Hagar, his wife's slave. Abraham had a son and he probably thought that would be OK with God. Guess again. Because of his actions things actually went wrong and people got hurt.

Centuries later a man named Moses would climb a mountain and confront God. The people of Israel were slaves in Egypt, waiting for a deliverer. And they waited about 400 years. That's not a good thing. Shouldn't God have set them free a lot sooner than that? I'm sure people were feeling like God was waiting too long.

But eventually God spoke to Moses and said, "I will send you Moses. You will go and deliver my people." And Moses says, "How can I do this? I am slow of speech." Moses may have had some type of speech problem. That certainly doesn't sound like the kind of person who should be speaking for God. It sounds like God goofed again. Or did he?

And again, centuries later, the prophet Jeremiah found himself in a very difficult position. Babylon had conquered his country. The temple of God had been ransacked, the treasures stolen, and people were taken away into exile. It was a dark time for the people. So the Lord spoke to Jeremiah and Jeremiah sent a letter to the people in exile. He told them to settle down, build a home and have a family, because you won't be coming back for 70 years.

That's when a man named Hananiah confronted Jeremiah and told him, "You are wrong. God has told me that in 2 years the people and the treasures will return from exile. Two years, not seventy."

And when Jeremiah heard this he said, "**Amen! May the Lord do so**." Jeremiah, the prophet of God, is telling this false prophet, "I hope you're right. I want to be wrong." But in the end, who was right? It was Jeremiah.

Throughout the centuries people have been expecting one thing and God does another. God does what people are not expecting and often what they do not welcome. But in the end it's always the same; God gives what people NEED, not what they want. What God does the things that fit into God's plans, not our plans.

Two thousand years ago Jesus went to the temple one day. The Passover celebration was at hand and it was at this time of year that people were especially hoping for a Messiah, a savior who would deliver them from the Romans. Not everyone was looking for a warrior Messiah but quite a few were. Most were looking for a king who would conquer the enemy and lead them to freedom.

So Jesus finally visited Jerusalem. He was in the temple grounds and it was the right time of year. Now would be a good time for a Messiah to appear and eliminate the Romans. But instead of attacking Rome Jesus attacked the temple. Jesus attacked the priests and the leaders who proclaimed the faith. Jesus made a whip out of cords and started to whip people out of the temple. This seems to be rather uncharacteristic of Jesus, but a whip is often seen as a symbol of judgment. Rather than judge the enemy Jesus judged the temple and the people in the temple. God's house is to be a house of prayer, a place of holiness. These people are selling sacrificial animals in the temple. People were doing business and seeking profits in the house of God. And it was forbidden to pay the temple tax with Roman coins, so people were exchanging their money for shekels. And naturally the money changers were charging a fee for this service. There were people on the grounds of God's holy temple exploiting other people for money. And chances are the priests were getting a kickback from the money changers. What has God said about things like this? "Thou shalt not steal."

Instead of calling for a war on Rome Jesus called for a war on sin, a war on corruption and a war on hypocrisy. He called for a war for holiness in the human heart and soul and a war for genuine worship and real faith in God. And these demands did not set well with many people.

When we approach God one of the hardest things to do is see beyond our current understanding of God. Whether we like to admit it or not most of us put God in a box. We expect God to act a certain way. We expect the truth to be our idea of truth. But, in the end, God behaves in ways we do not expect and do not understand.

In the second century, on a plaster wall outside Rome, someone scratched a drawing of a man on a cross, but the image has the head of a donkey. There is a caption that reads, "Alexamenos worships his God." That's obviously an insult to Christianity and it is exactly how people looked at the crucifixion. The idea of a God-man who was crucified and died was idiocy to them just as it is idiocy to many people today.

Greeks sought wisdom. For them the notion of a God taking human form to die flew in the face of wisdom. But where does human wisdom come from? It comes from very flawed and imperfect human beings. Won't flawed people have flawed wisdom?

Jews wanted signs and Jesus seemed like the wrong kind of sign. How could the Son of God have been treated in such a horrible way? How could people have failed to see his greatness? God should come to destroy sin, not be destroyed by sinners.

But demanding a sign shows a lack of faith. We won't believe it unless we see something. And when we do see something what if it's NOT what we expect to see? Then we won't believe it. Should we insist God provide a better sign or should we be looking for what God is saying?

Faith is about believing even when we do not see. Faith is believing even when it seems silly. Didn't God work in odd ways with Abraham? A 100-year-old man and his 90-year-old wife shouldn't be having children. How about Moses? A man who stutters seems like an unlikely voice for God.

So the cross is foolishness to those who seek wisdom. And it's ridiculous to those seeking signs. But apparently the foolishness of God is greater than human wisdom and the weakness of God is greater than human strength.

The cross of Jesus does what no wisdom or signs can do; it saves.

The God of love lays down his life for us just as parents would lay down their lives for their children.

The sacrifice of God buys salvation for all, and the sign from God is the resurrection.

Does God do the wrong thing or are we always looking for the wrong thing? Years ago I was challenged with the question, "Are we really seeking God's will, or do we just hope God sees things our way?"

We need to push ourselves to see things God's way especially when it's a teaching we don't like. We must not rely on our own wisdom and understanding. We need to open our minds to a greater reality. We need to truly seek God's ways, not our own ways.

We need to put our faith in God, especially when what God is asking seems so wrong.

Let us open our minds a little wider and look for a God far beyond what we've ever imagined.

In Jesus' name

Temptation

Luke 4:1-13

There's a story of a man who searched the internet and found a wish website. He clicked on a lamp 3 times and a genie appeared in his room. But this Genie only granted 1 wish. So the man had a lot to think about. A LOT!

If you only had 1 wish to make what would it be? Think about that for a minute.

The man took several days to really, really think. He realized he could wish for money, or fame, or great health and long life. Or he could wish for a beautiful wife. Or maybe he could even wish to become leader of the world. But he thought about it and realized it would be extremely selfish to have a HUGE opportunity like this and just wish for some personal gain.

So he thought a while longer. He knew there was great suffering in the world. So he thought about making it so everyone would live forever; never die. But then he thought if no one ever died but people kept having babies the world would be overrun with people in no time, so we'd have to stop having babies. Then he tried to imagine a world where there were no babies or children. How sad would that world be.

Then he thought about how ending war and violence would be great. Imagine no one ever killing anyone ever again. Imagine no one ever going to war again. That would be a great world. But then he realized if he did that, he would be taking away everyone's freedom of choice. In order for us to really be human we have to have freedom. And to be truly free we have to have choices, even bad choices.

Then he thought about ending disease and hunger. But soon realized it wouldn't be long before the earth was again overrun with people.

He started to realize if someone took away every obstacle in the world what would there be to learn? How would the human race grow and become a better people if someone just magically made all problems vanish?

So, what would you wish for? What should we wish for?

I know some people object to this story because magic and genies do not represent Christian beliefs or values. In fact they conflict with some biblical standards. True! But as we read the Bible, we find Jesus facing a somewhat similar situation.

The story goes that after Jesus was baptized, he went into the desert. It's a very common image to see a holy man go into the desert or wilderness to prepare for God's great work. They need to step away from this world and focus on the other. They need to face themselves, their strengths and weaknesses, their past and God's call. It's a time for fasting, denying their own needs, so they can simply focus on God.

One day Moses climbed a mountain, alone, because he saw a burning bush. Sometime later, after he led the people out of Egypt, he went back to the mountain, this time for a long while. He had to go and wait upon the Lord.

When Elijah was running from Jezebel he ran into the desert. Then he ran to the mountain of God itself. There he hid, and waited, and prayed, until God revealed himself.

So Jesus went into the desert before he began his ministry. Even Jesus needed to face himself and seek an encounter with God.

But one of the things he had to face was the ultimate temptations, brought to him by the ultimate tempter. If Jesus really was the Son of God, then Satan would have to pull out his best prizes in order to lead him to sin.

In the Bible Satan means "accuser" or "slanderer" but is sometimes known as the "tempter." It was the serpent that accused God of lying and then tempted Eve to eat the fruit. So the serpent has often been identified as Satan. Whether that is literally true or not the Bible talks of a tempter, an accuser, and an adversary of God.

Like the great prophets Jesus fasted. And after a time he was very hungry. So comes the first temptation. "If you are the Son of God, then command the stones to become loaves of bread." In the beginning God spoke and a universe came into being. All God did was speak and it happened. Surely if Jesus is the Son of God he can speak, and stone will turn to bread. Hunger can make people do crazy things, even evil things. All Jesus needed to do was say the word and his own physical needs would be met.

But Jesus has other things in mind. He did not come to earth to use his power to fill his own needs. And he is not in the wilderness to eat. He is in the wilderness for a higher purpose. He has come for God and not bread. Man cannot live on bread alone. Man must live on the word of God. Jesus is in the wilderness because he hungers for God as we should all hunger for God. God should be our highest drive. Not money, not even food; God should be our food.

So Jesus passed this test. It's time for the next. There is some difference in the gospels as to what order the temptations came, but there are two more.

Satan takes Jesus to the pinnacle of the temple in Jerusalem. Jesus is not standing on the roof of the temple itself, but on a corner of the temple grounds and it's quite a drop to the rocks below. It would almost certainly be fatal. So the devil tempts Jesus to jump. This is the temple grounds. There would be many people on the temple grounds. He would have plenty of witnesses. They would see a man jumping off the pinnacle. Imagine what people would have thought if the man jumped and he was not harmed. Or what people would have thought if they saw angels grab this man and carry him away. They would have screamed, "It's a miracle." They would have honored and followed that man.

But again that is not why Jesus came to earth. He didn't come to show off. He wasn't supposed to use his power to create followers. Jesus wouldn't use his powers to glorify himself. He would use his powers to help people.

And what if Jesus did jump expecting God to save him? We are called on to have faith but that doesn't mean we should do something that could lead to a tragedy. It's one thing to be on a plane while it's crashing and pray to God. It's another thing to deliberately crash the plane and see what happens. Jesus said, "Thou shalt not test the Lord."

So then the devil pulls out his very best offer. Satan shows Jesus all the world, all the kingdoms, all the land, and he makes Jesus an offer. "All of this I will give to you if you will bow down and worship me." Try to imagine saying 'NO' to that.

Here is a golden opportunity to save the world. Jesus could take every human being and just hand them over to God now and forever. There'd be no need to be crucified. No need for a difficult ministry. All he would have to do is bend a knee to Satan. Isn't this a good example of, "the greater good?"

In Cecil B Demille's movie, "The 10 Commandments," there's a scene where Moses is talking to Nefertiti. She advises him to keep his mouth shut, not admit to being a Hebrew, and then Moses would probably be chosen as the next Pharaoh. As Pharaoh he could simply set his people free and let them worship whoever or whatever they wanted, and after that he would still be a King with great power over thousands.

That sounds like a great thing. But that's not how God would work the delivery from Egypt.

And that's not how Jesus would bring salvation to the world. If Jesus said yes to this he would be bowing to Satan, something no one should ever do for any reason.

And he would also be taking away our free will. One of the things that makes us human is our ability to choose. God did not create us to be robots who have no choice but to obey. God made us with free will. And God didn't make us all perfect so that all evil would be abhorrent to us. No! God gave us enough of a sinful nature that evil can be very tempting. And God gave us the right to choose; the right to say yes or no to God. God wants us to follow him because it's the right choice.

If Jesus just took Satan's offer and handed the world over to God there would be no choices, no freedoms, no alternatives. We would no longer be human. And that is not how God made the world.

Many ask the question, "was this story literal or was it a metaphor?" Did Jesus actually struggle with a real being or was this symbolic? I think the answer is, "does it really matter?" The fact is Jesus had to face some hard temptations in this world and some hard choices.

Have you ever watched some television news story about someone who commits a horrific crime and think, "someone should shoot him and save us all a lot of trouble"? Haven't we all had a thought like that a few times in our lives? It does make sense in so many ways, but is that what God wants? No.

Have we ever had the temptation to do something the easy way? I'm sure we all have and sometimes the easy way is fine. But how often is the easy way the best way for everyone?

Jesus said "No" to the greatest temptations of all. We preach of a savior, Jesus Christ, who turned aside from all evil. He was the only person who ever lived a sinless life.

But he knew what sin was. He knew how tempting evil can be. Jesus is one of us. When we say, "Jesus is with us," it's true. Jesus is with us in our suffering and temptation because he went through it himself.

When temptation comes our way, and it will, we need to be ready. We need to face our own weaknesses that will lead us into strong temptation. We need to face the evil that lives in us all and fight it.

And when we fail, someone is there ready to forgive. Someone knows we are far from perfect, so he is very forgiving.

We will fail sometimes. When we do someone is there ready to pick us up, forgive us, cleanse us, and send us back into the world. Hopefully when we fail, we learn a lesson, grow in faith, find a way around temptation, and not fail again the next time.

Even if we fail 1000 times, someone is there for us, someone loves us, and someone will see us through. Jesus Christ our tempted but sinless savior.

In his name:

Watch Your Mouth

James 3:1-12

When we were kids and people were calling us names, what did our parents teach us? "Sticks and stones may break my bones, but names will never hurt me."

Then you grow up and learn that everyday thousands of psychologists all across the world are treating people with psychological problems because they have been horribly scarred by words.

Women who are physically abused are almost always abused verbally and most of them report the verbal abuse was even worse than the fists.

And when a child is told over and over again that they are bad or worthless, especially when it comes from someone they love, it makes very deep and long-lasting scars.

Bruises heal fairly quickly but sometimes the mind doesn't heal for years, if ever.

Today we live in a society where businesses have to remind their employees to watch what they say every minute of every day. If you say the wrong word, and people take offense, the business can be in trouble. Quite often businesses and employees are all told "words have power," and they always did.

According to the Bible God saw that the earth was dark, and God said, "Let there be light." And there was light. All God had to do was speak and it happened. This has actually led some theologians to believe that the very heart of all reality is words. God spoke and it came into existence.

And when we read through the Bible, we see the term "the Word of God" is a common and essential theme. If God says it, it's important. The Bible testifies loud and clear about the power of words.

When we look at history and ask the question, "What things have pushed history forward?" there are many answers. But we dare not ignore the power of words, both written and spoken. How did great leaders influence their people? Quite often by words. Sometimes they used fancy words and eloquent speech. Sometimes they used simple everyday but delivered with a powerful voice and fiery speech. Words changed the world.

In the middle and late 19th century great thinkers like Karl Marx and Friedrich Nietzsche were hard at work thinking, writing, and speaking their words. They were just two philosophers, 2 great thinkers, in a world full of thousands of people who wanted to be the great minds of the day. It's so easy to imagine them simply disappearing into history like so many others. Instead their words endured. Their words had an impact on millions and influenced history. These two philosophers helped to mold much of the 20th century with just their words. **Words have power.**

James knew this when he wrote his letter. The tongue is just a little bit of flesh. A small muscle in a large body. But quite often small things have far more power than you know. The tongue can be a great gift, or a deadly weapon. A little spark can start a fire that burns down a forest. So the wrong word can have a powerful impact.

Jesus knew this. He warned warns us about careless words.

Matthew 5: 22 - "**whosoever shall say to his brother, Raca, shall be in danger of the council:**" Raca literally means "empty head." Does that sound kind of familiar? Kind of like stupid, idiot, brainless… I know we're all guilty of it. I'm guilty to. I'm not trying to shame anyone, and I don't believe we will literally face a courtroom for calling someone an empty head. Jesus often spoke in extremes to make his point clear. He is trying to drive the point home as hard as he can that words have power and should be used wisely.

Hitler used his fiery rhetoric and words that appealed to the widespread hatred and prejudice that was common in Germany in the 1930s. He used his words to incite the hatred and unite good people into an evil empire. As James said, the tongue can be a restless evil full of deadly poison. Unspeakable evil happened because of someone's deadly tongue.

This is why James tried to warn people about the tongue. He tried to focus on what words can do. "The tongue also is a fire, a world of evil among the parts of the body. It corrupts the whole body, sets the whole course of one's life on fire, and is itself set on fire by hell." There can be hell in the human tongue.

But he also tells us to imagine what can happen if we could tame the tongue. That is hard to do because it is so easy to slip and say the wrong thing. It's so easy to let the tongue start moving before the brain wakes up. But imagine what could happen if we mastered it.

Why were people so amazed by Jesus? Here was a carpenter's son from a tiny little town. He was a nobody. But the Bible says quite often people were impressed by him because he spoke as if he were someone who "spoke with authority." Jesus wasn't just quoting scripture. He spoke as if he had personal knowledge and personal experience regarding the scripture. He spoke as one whose words were true and worthy of admiration.

It's the difference between reading the book and being the expert who wrote the book. It's the difference between reading about a certain surgery and being the one who invented and perfected that surgery. Jesus is the authority. Jesus knows what he's talking about because the Word of God is in him, not just in the person he's quoting.

And quite often the words he chose were not all that amazing. Jesus said "The kingdom of God is like…" something common and every day; seeds, a man catching fish, a woman making some bread or a shepherd looking for a sheep. The words were common, the words were simple, but the result was to reveal incredible truth. People learned about God because of the words Jesus spoke. People learned about how they should be living their lives because of words. You don't need big, fancy, complex words to make a difference. Even simple little words can have power.

James chapter 3 talks about all the things the tongue can do. Then he says something else that's kind of strange. He compares the tongue to a bit in a horse's mouth, or the rudder of a ship. We use these fairly small things to control and guide something notably bigger. It seems like he is telling us the tongue helps to control our direction. That's a little odd since it's the brain that guides the tongue and the brain that's supposed to guide our direction, not the tongue. Perhaps James wasn't speaking literally, but then again maybe he was.

Imagine someone who is constantly telling himself or herself that they are stupid, worthless, or whatever. A person who keeps saying these things over and over will believe them. So a counselor might give them something else to say. "Every morning when you wake up, and every night when you go to bed, and every time you feel worthless you speak, out loud, a positive affirmation. Like, 'I am a good person,' or 'I am smart and capable.'" Even at the times when they really do not believe it, they are to keep saying it. Eventually the message starts to sink in. Instead of the brain telling the tongue what to say, the tongue starts to tell the brain what to think. And a person who starts to think positive thoughts is a life that will head in a new direction. So the tongue can indeed act as a rudder for your life.

Imagine what can happen when we start to tell ourselves, "I am a child of God." "I was born to do God's great work." What happens when we tell ourselves, "Jesus died for me"? When we start to fill our hearts and minds with these words it makes a difference. When we start to look at ourselves the way God looks at us the world can look so different. When we say the right words to ourselves the words can become a positive guide in our lives. These are ways to use your tongue as a rudder that guides you to follow God's currents instead of earthly currents that will always send you to the rocks.

And when we say these words to other people it can also have a powerful, healing and life changing effect on others.

I once took a friend's son to a park with a very tall slide. He was only about 2 years old, and he really wanted to slide down that slide. But he got about ¾ of the way up and got scared. It was pretty tall for such a small boy. But I stood there on the ground beneath him, and I said, "You can do it. I believe in you." And he finished climbing and slid down the slide. And I was there to say, "Way to go. Proud of you." I doubt he remembers that but hopefully somewhere in his mind he will know someone out there believes in him. Hopefully my words are hiding in the back of his mind somewhere.

And hopefully we can find words like those to say to one another today.

Why are so many churches hurting? There are a lot of reasons. In some churches one of the reasons for a large decline in attendance happened because someone said the wrong thing. Feelings got hurt and people broke away. That is sad. As Christians we should know that we are all very flawed. We should know people will say things they really shouldn't say.

We need to take a few insults or some careless words and not let them eat us up or drive us out of the church. This is God's church; this is your church, and this is my church. It is not the church of just one person who said the wrong thing. We need to look beyond that. We need to remember we are all human and humans make mistakes. As Christians we must be ready to forgive.

But if we mind our tongue there will be less to forgive.

And what about the people who do not come to our church at all? What does it say to them when they hear about fights, arguments, and divisions popping up in churches because someone said the wrong thing? Would you want to go to a church like that? We need to watch our tongues for our own sake and for the sake of our brothers and sisters in the church, but we should also be wise for the sake of those NOT in the church. The words we say are part of our witness. We are supposed to be using our tongue to bless God, not curse people who are made in the image of God.

Even when we are angry, even when we are hurt, even what something really terrible has happened, we can find words that build up instead of tearing down.

Would you like to build up your church? Maybe we can start by trying to say the right thing today. "God Bless you. God loves you. You are a beautiful creation of God. God believes in you, and I believe in you. "

Say words like these to yourself and to one another, and maybe your ship will start sailing into more blessed waters.

In Jesus' name

My Personal Funeral Experiences:

It has been said, "Some of the greatest ministry takes place in the funeral home and at the graveside." Whoever said that was right. Although funerals have to be my least favorite pastoral duty they can be powerful avenues of faith and ministry. When the grim reaper appears it gives us great reasons to think about life and all that truly matters in life. Many people have said to me, "I couldn't have gotten through this without my faith." So God can truly be seen and appreciated standing by the coffin or the tombstone.

Forgive me if it seems like I am boasting but people have told me from early in my ministry that my three greatest gifts as pastor are preaching, singing, and funeral services. People say I have this ability to take a human being's life and bring out some of the best aspects of the person. In fact at my own mother's funeral my best friend brought his girlfriend. She complimented me for what I said and told me, "even though I never met your mother I feel like I know her."

I'm sure it isn't typical to ask someone, "what's your secret for making a good funeral sermon," but it might be something pastors would want to know. No one has ever asked me about how I do it.

When writing a story, quite often you find something that inspires you, catches your imagination, and you just have to let your imagination take over. Sometimes you just follow your heart and let the story flow.

When writing a sermon, my Uncle John taught me to study the scripture and ask three questions:

- What is the scripture saying?

- How does it relate to the world today?

- What do the church members need to hear?

Then you pray for guidance. Then you see what you and God can work out together.

That usually works well for a Sunday morning sermon but not so much for a funeral.

When it comes to funerals I do have a formula for a healing sermon and it is very simple.

I once read, "everyone has a sermon in them; a preacher is someone who knows how to tell their sermon 100 different ways." So, when it comes to the deceased I ask myself one question, "What was this person's sermon? What was God telling us through this person's life?"

No matter how well I knew the deceased I always make sure I talk to the family and listen to them (especially if I did not know the deceased). I try to look at their life so I can understand who and what they were. I ask the question, "What was God trying to tell us through this person's life?" And from there the funeral sermon often flows fairly easily.

Please notice I said **"Often,"** but not **"Always."** I have found myself facing many difficult funerals and it is especially from those moments I'd like to share some of the things I've learned and messages God has put into my heart.

****

I took a course called Clinical Pastoral Education in the early 1990s. It's kind of hard to describe all that CPE involves and all I learned from it. But one important lesson I learned was that mourning is a good thing. It certainly does not feel like it when we are experiencing it but there is a purpose in mourning.

When we lose someone we value it is painful. Mourning is a God given gift and a God given **RIGHT** for all of us. It is a blessing to mourn so we can work out the pain, learn from the pain, grow from the pain, and come through it to a better understanding of life and God.

Let no one discourage you from mourning. Let no one shame or embarrass you for mourning. Let no one tell you how to mourn. Just shed your tears and let them be your special tears. Tears can be a great gift from God.

****

I was often uncomfortable with funerals when I began my ministry. But one day I had an experience that helped me get over a lot of the stress that comes from funerals.

During my first assignment as pastor I was asked to do a funeral for a man who lived into his nineties. He had a daughter who lived a fair distance from town so his landlady was asked to make the arrangements.

She didn't have too many personal stories about his life. Much of what she knew about him came from her personal experiences that only went back a few years. But she knew the man started working after he graduated High School and worked most of his life. During those years he got married, had one daughter, and was a good father and husband. The daughter grew up, had a couple children and he was a good grandfather to them. His wife died shortly after he retired but he continued to live his life as a good man.

Then one day he moved into an apartment where the landlady welcomed him and introduced him to her family. She had two young sons and soon he became a grandfather to both of them.

In all, it doesn't sound like he had an extraordinary life. He never built a great invention. He never wrote a great novel. In many ways his life was rather ordinary.

But for his daughter, her children, his landlady, her children, and others, he was a very special man. He was a kind and loving man who did a lot of good. He was available for other people. No one had a bad thing to say about him. Then when he was in his nineties he died peacefully in his sleep. What more can be said? In so many ways his life was complete.

That's the day I became far more comfortable with funerals. I've known for a long time death is a natural part of life, but this is the first time I really felt it. I felt some level of peace I had never felt with a funeral because, "his life was complete." He lived a long, full, genuine life and overall a happy life, and now it was over.

Even though most of us will not live into our 90s most of us will live into our 70s and 80s. Even though most of us will not be the great novelist or scientist or President of the United States, during our time on earth we can all live good, kind, honest, genuine lives. We may not be "great" as the world sees greatness, but we can be great to the people around us.

This is why at a funeral I often use the scripture from Job 42; "So Job died old and full of days."

****

When it comes to emotional pain, especially the kind you find in funerals, I have often had this deep desire to help the families in grief. I imagine most people can understand what I mean because I know many people have the same desire to help someone in pain.

It took me a while to learn the lesson that you can't take away someone's pain. It is impossible. There are no rituals or magic words that end the pain.

But, one day, I had a conversation with my Uncle Jay about my father's death. The words he spoke to me are about as close to "magic words for a funeral" as I have ever heard.

My uncle's own father died while he was quite young himself. After the funeral he noticed that his grandmother never seemed to stop mourning. In fact it seemed to him like she mourned for her son until she herself was laid to rest.

But his grandfather never seemed to shed a tear.

This obviously confused my uncle so he talked with his grandfather one day. His grandfather told him, "Not a day goes by that your grandmother does not say, 'God, why did you take away my son?' But not a day goes by when I do not say, 'Thank you God for what I had.'"

It is painful to know that life is finite, in fact even people who live to be 100 can still feel like life is short. We need to remember **NO ONE is given to us forever**. In some ways our loved ones are not a "gift" from God. People are "on loan" to us. Sooner or later everyone we love will be gone and we will be gone leaving a hole in the lives of the people who love us.

Wouldn't it be nice if we really remembered how short our lives can be and how precious each moment can be?

Wouldn't it be great if we would remember how much we have now and give thanks, because so many of the great things in our lives, including the people we love the most, will be gone eventually.

When our loved ones are gone it will hurt and it is our God given right to mourn. But, in time, we should remember the good times, those special memories, and be thankful for what we had instead of just mourning what we've lost.

****

One of the most difficult funerals I ever had was the death of a young girl. The night before the funeral I sat up late sweating. What words can I come up with on a day like this?

Then, I can truly say, God put the right story into my heart.

I once lived in northern Michigan right on Lake Superior. I often walked the beach on nice nights. It can be a very beautiful and calming experience. One very clear night I laid in the sand looking up at the stars. You can see stars far better in northern Michigan than in many parts of America. I laid there, enjoying the night, very happy to see the stars.

Suddenly a bright meteor went streaking across the sky. I jumped up to get a better look at it but it was gone very quickly. I probably saw it for less than 2 seconds but it made quite an impression in my heart. I laid back and looked at the stars again but they suddenly seemed disappointing. They weren't as exciting as that one meteor.

This is where my sermon began. This child was a fireball that caught our attention. She was only with us for a short time but in that short time she meant so much to all of us, brought such joy and excitement to all of us, made our hearts jump, and suddenly the world does seem to be a little empty without her.

We need to mourn such a painful loss. But when the mourning is done we can smile and remember those little fireballs that really lit up our skies, even if just for a moment.

****

I have officiated at many funerals for people I never met. One such service involved a widow and her children. I met the family, discussed the date and time for the funeral and any other arrangements they might need from me. Then I began to ask about the woman herself. As always I tried to listen to the family and learn about the deceased.

For a few tense minutes there was silence in the room. The family finally started divulging a few facts about her but it was hard for them. Finally the oldest sadly shared that she was not a good mother. It was hard for them to grow up under her. She was often a cold mother. She apparently had a lot of anger and negativity in her life that she took it out on her own family. These adult children had a hard time saying nice things about their own mother.

That's when I said, "People aren't usually cranky for the fun of it."

Most of the time when people are angry, difficult to get along with or have a very negative outlook on life, it's because some bad things happened to them. Childhood trauma, like abuse or serious losses, can leave you with lifelong pains and negative attitude. Growing up in poverty, or with parents who are very negative themselves, can bring out negative attitudes in children.

Even without abuse or serious problems in childhood, life can bring difficulties.

Life can be very unfair. When children go to school they will often find someone far better at a subject than they are no matter how hard they study, and it can be very frustrating. Some of us are simply born with the potential to be better at some things than other people.

Some people will be born to be taller or with the potential to be more muscular, and quite often the tall and strong will victimize the shorter and weaker. Some of us will be more attractive than others. And some people will be born into poverty, violence, abuse, or other serious problems. Life can be unfair and it can lead us into anger and frustration, which can lead to negativity.

So if you ever have a funeral for someone who was known for their negative attitude, or a cold personality, try to remember they were probably not born to be negative. Chances are they faced some troubles in their life and it hurt them deeply.

Most of the time negative people hate themselves as much as we might hate them. Most of the time negative people are victims who need our sympathy and love.

****

If I had to choose which kind of funerals are the worst I would say funerals for children are the worst, but suicides are a very close second.

When a friend or loved one commits suicide it can feel like a kick in the stomach. It can feel like they are telling you, "I don't care how much you love me. I'm going to hurt you like you've never been hurt before." I know. It has happened to me.

We need to remember this is not the case. Sometimes people carry deep pain in their hearts and for some reason it's hard to open up about it. It's a secret they keep buried and like a lot of secrets, sooner or later, it explodes out of you.

People do not commit suicide to spite us. People commit suicide because they are in pain. I once had a thought that if a person who was contemplating suicide could look at the future and see what how much agony it would bring to their family, maybe they'd think twice. I have since learned that is not the case. Even that kind of motivation won't stop people in that much pain.

When we experience a suicide we must not blame ourselves. Their choice is not a reflection of our love or feelings for others. Sometimes even people who are very well loved take their own lives. They felt pain and emptiness that sometimes does not make sense.

It's not our fault if we failed to see the signs. Sometimes even experts can't see the signs. The only way to save someone truly intent on suicide is to lock them up. That may keep them alive but it doesn't end their pain.

For those of us who are left behind we can blame ourselves, second guess ourselves and wonder about "what if." It will get us nowhere. We start to heal by understanding there really is nothing we could do. We are not responsible for someone's tragic decision. All we can do is mourn our loss and hold them in our hearts as much as we hold anyone else we lose.

****

One thing that can make suicides even more painful for families is when people come forward and say, "people who commit suicide go straight to Hell."

Families mourning their loss do not need to hear something like that. It is also probably untrue.

Jesus said there is only one unforgiveable sin; blasphemy against the Holy Spirit. (Mark 3:28-30) There is a great deal of debate about what "Blasphemy against the Holy Spirit" really means. The message and the exact meaning are a little cryptic but I have never heard anyone say, "Blasphemy against the Holy Spirit is suicide." I have not once heard that interpretation.

Jesus was very interested in healing pain, not punishing it with damnation.

****

I once officiated for a funeral where a couple had to face the horrible reality that their grown son had murdered his wife then committed suicide.

Of course my deepest sympathies went out to the family of the wife. I called and offered my condolences. It's horrible to lose a child. It is far worse to lose your child to murder, especially when the murderer is the person who is supposed to love your child the most.

But the family of the man who did this was also hurting. Not only were they devastated by their loss, they were also devastated to know their son could do something like this. Why did he do this? What evil grabbed his heart to make him do such a despicable thing?

I spent a lot of time with the family. I saw no evidence they were an abusive or highly dysfunctional family and the man's sister seemed healthy and well adjusted. That makes this man's actions all the more mysterious and tragic.

Once again I found myself facing a very hard situation; what do I say about a man who killed his own spouse then himself?

Fortunately I had learned a valuable truth shortly before this event. Someone once said, "Each of us is more than the worst thing we've ever done."

It's one of those sayings that I'm sure a lot of people will attribute to one great thinker or another. We may never know exactly who said it first, but it is the truth. If people were to judge us by our worst moments what would the world think of us?

I started with this truth and the rest of the message, and my time with the family, flowed out and became a source of healing for them.

In fact one day they reported to me they had given their lives to Christ.

Quite a few people have come forward for an altar call after a worship service and proclaimed their new devotion to Christ. For some their declaration is quite genuine. For others it is short lived.

It was my great honor to see that their decision was real and long lasting. I saw the change in them and was able to celebrate it with them.

As I said, God can do great work at the graveside.

****

One of my favorite scripture readings comes from John chapter 9; Jesus heals a man who was born blind. I often use it at funerals and on other occasions.

The disciples asked Jesus, "Why was he born blind? Was it his sins or the sins of his parents?"

Jesus answered them, "This man did not sin, nor did his parents. He was born blind so the works of God could be seen in his life."

I often think of Helen Keller when I read those words. Although she was not born blind and deaf her maladies came on her at such an early age it was as if she were born with them. Helen suffered greatly. But it was because of her suffering and her struggles to live a reasonably normal life that she became such an outspoken public speaker and deeply involved in social issues. Her suffering helped to create such an amazing human being that we truly can see God worked through her in her suffering.

In the book, "War of the Worlds," by H.G. Wells, the earth is subjected to an invasion by aliens from Mars. Humanity fought back bravely with all their military might but it was useless. In the end the aliens were brought down by earthly bacteria and viruses. H. G Wells concluded the story with these words:

"By the toll of a billion deaths man has bought his birthright of the earth, and it is his against all comers; it would still be his were the Martians ten times as mighty as they are. For neither do men live nor die in vain."

Untold billions of people have suffered from sicknesses over the centuries. Billions more have suffered torture, war and oppression. Human history is written with blood. It is comforting and in fact something to celebrate to think that none of these people lived or died in vain. In some ways we have become the people we are because of our own pain. Pain that can make us better Christians and the pain can help God's work become more visible in us and through us.

****

One of the last funerals I officiated at in Michigan was for an older woman who died of natural causes.

Her family told me one of their fond memories took place on Christmas day. She would often try to sing "Silent Night" in the original German. She would get through a few sentences and say, "something like that."

So, for her funeral, as I gave my message, I mentioned this fond memory and I began to sing. Just by coincidence I know the first verse of "Silent Night" in German. I felt bad at first because I moved the family to tears. But, as usual, those tears are healing. They thanked me profusely for what I did and how special I made the service.

Putting in a special memory can really bring healing into a lot of pain.

(And is it really just a coincidence that I just happened to know the song in German?)

The Legend of the Snowsnake

The northern wood is a place where the winters are long and cold. The snow falls deep and only the strong and clever animals survive. It's so cold in winter that no snakes can slither about.

At least not anymore.

Once, long ago, there was a deadly snake that lived in the cold northern woods. The great white Snowsnakes would come out of their dens in the white of winter to hunt in the ice and snow.

Snowsnakes were the terror of the northern woods; so dangerous that even the great northern bears feared them. But in time a new creature came to the north, something far deadlier than even the great serpents; people came. It wasn't long before men killed the Snowsnakes until there was only one left.

One cold winter day, the last Snowsnake had to fight a powerful wolverine. The snake beat the wolverine but he was badly hurt by the beast's claws.

The snake lay bleeding on the ground. He would have died except a little boy came along and found the snake. He knew Snowsnakes were the deadliest animals in the north, but the boy felt sorry for him. He picked up the snake and carried him home. His mother was terrified when she saw her son carry the snake into her home. But the boy cried and begged his mother to help the poor snake. So the boy and his mother bandaged the snake, fed him milk, and laid him in a box of straw. Many people don't like snakes, but you might want to know snakes don't like people either. But the Snowsnake knew the boy and his mother were only trying to help him, so the snake did not bite.

As the days went on, the snake began to recover. The mother was terrified of the snake, but the little boy would feed him, sit beside him, and told him the stories his mother had taught him. Snakes aren't supposed to be deaf, but somehow the snake began to understand what the boy was saying.

The mother would read to her son from a book called the Bible. In one story she told him of the evil things snakes had done. In the beginning, God made man to be good, and man lived in peace with God. But the snake came to tempt the woman and the man in the Garden of Eden, and they sinned a great sin, so the man, the woman, and the snake were punished.

"O sure, blame me for everything," said the snake.

But a few days later the woman turned to another part of the book. She began to read about a man who was called Jesus. Jesus was called the Son of God, and one day he died on a cross. But, because he died on the cross, all the people of the world could be forgiven for all the evil things they do, and so people could live with God forever. Even the snake was very surprised when he heard this story. And the little boy said, "God forgives us when we do bad things?"

"Yes," said his mother.

"So why can't God forgive the snakes?" the little boy asked. His mother was surprised when her son said this, and she didn't know what to say.

A few nights later, the snake watched as the boy and his mother did a very strange thing. They brought a small pine tree into the house. They said it was to celebrate Christmas, the day the Son of God was born. And the snake thought, "First they build houses so they don't have to live in the woods. Now they're planting trees in the living room. Humans are very weird."

The snake didn't understand how you celebrate a birthday with a tree but one day he got out of the box and he found it fun to climb the tree and sit in its branches. The boy watched as the snake sat in the branches of the tree and how his white scales shimmered in the light of the fire. "Doesn't he look pretty mommy?" the boy said. His mother was still frightened by the snake but she had to admit he did look kind of pretty as he lay in the branches with his scales glistened in the light.

On Christmas Eve, as the boy and his mother slept, a great Kodiak bear came into the house. The snake saw the beast come in as he lay in the branches of the tree. "What are you doing in my house?" said the snake.

The bear growled at him, "I am hungry. I haven't eaten for days."

"There's no food for you here," the snake hissed, "now get out."

But the bear growled at him, "Then I will eat the boy and his mother tonight. Now stay out of my way."

The snake was still weak but he slithered across the floor and stopped in front of the bedroom door. "No one is going to kill a good Christian mother and child on Christmas Eve. Not while I'm in the house."

The snake lunged at the bear, but the bear quickly stepped back. The snake fought bravely but he was weak and slow. The bear brought his great paw down and crushed the snake's body with one blow. But the Snowsnake somehow found enough strength to raise his head from the floor one last time and plunged his fangs into the bear's paw. The bear howled in agony and ran off into the woods and the last Snowsnake quietly laid down his head for the last time.

The boy and his mother hid in their room, terrified to come out until the sun rose in the morning. When they came out, they found the snake dead on the floor. Early on a cold Christmas morning, mother and son, with tears in their eyes, carried their friend out into the woods and buried the last Snowsnake in the snow.

But an angel of the Lord saw what the snake had done. He carried the snake to heaven and placed him before the throne of God.

The Lord said, "Long ago, the snake tempted my children, Adam and Eve, and caused them to sin. That is why I cursed the serpents and that is why they crawl the ground and lick the dust of the road. But you, as cursed as you are, you did a wonderful thing. You gave your life to save the lives of others because you knew they were my children."

"Once I sent my Son to save humanity. He gave his life to forgive them their sins and to give them a way to live forever, with me."

"So, for the sake of my Son Jesus, I forgive even the serpents for their sins. Snakes will always crawl the ground, but they are also the creation of God. As for you, my brave little friend, I have a special place for you. "

That is why, today, you will never see snakes on a cold winter day. But, if you look, whenever the snow falls and the wind blows, you may see snakelike tracks in the snow. That's a sign from God that someone is looking after you.

Sometimes in winter you will hear a gentle hiss as the wind blows, or you may feel a cold bite on your nose or feet. Don't be afraid, it's only the last Snowsnake, guarding all God's people who live in the cold, frozen north.

When you hang your shiny tinsel upon the Christmas tree, remember the shiny white snake who gave his life to save his friends.

And when you see the beauty of your Christmas tree, remember Jesus, born on a beautiful Christmas day. Remember the man who died on a cross, to save all God's people, so that we may all live with him, forever.

Those Who Were Not Wise

And so it came to pass that a young woman gave birth to a baby in a stable in the small town of Bethlehem. She wrapped him in swaddling clothes him and laid him in a manger because there was no room for them in the Inn.

That very night shepherds came to see the baby because an angel appeared to them in the fields and declared, "unto you, this night, in the town of Bethlehem, a savior has been born." So the shepherds came to honor their newborn savior.

Later, three wise men came from the east and asked, "Where is he who is born the King of the Jews." And the wise men searched until they found him. When they did, they knelt down and honored the newborn king.

Then the three wise men left Israel and returned home.

But these visitors would not be the last to come to the baby's cradle. Soon others came to see the newborn king, but most of them were not wise.

One day a king came to Bethlehem to see the baby. The king stood before the baby Jesus wearing his crown of gold and his finest robe. He looked down at him, knowing this baby would one day grow up to be a king. So the king said, "All my life I've dreamed of being a king. I have always wanted to live in a palace, wear the finest clothes, and lead a huge nation. Now I am a king with subjects and great wealth and power, but I am not happy. What is wrong?"

And the king looked at the baby, and Jesus showed him the future.

The king saw Jesus as a man. But "King Jesus" did not wear fine clothes, or live in a palace, or lead thousands of subjects.

King Jesus walked the land, preaching the word of God, sitting with the common people, eating ordinary food. He didn't demand the people serve him; he served them. He healed the sick, fed the hungry, comforted those who mourned, and told people to do the same.

After he had seen these things the king took off his crown and robe. He laid them on the ground before the baby and walked away. The king went forth to serve the needs of others, help others, and lead people by giving of himself.

Then a beautiful woman, wearing fine clothes and jewelry, went in and looked down at the baby. She said to him, "All I've ever wanted is to be loved. All my life I've tried to be good to people so they'd love me. I've done what people wanted, even doing things that are dishonorable, hoping someone would truly love me. But instead I feel dirty. People use me and people hurt me. Now people make fun of me, insult me, and call me unclean. What can I do?"

She looked at Jesus and Jesus showed her the future. Jesus showed her a woman caught in adultery. People said she was dirty, but Jesus told her she was forgiven. Jesus told her she was now clean. He told her she was also a child of God and she should act like a child of God.

After this the woman threw off her jewels and left the stable. She went out to live a righteous life. She went to live the way God had told her. In time she found other people who had also been cleaned by God. She found other people who truly did love her as God loved her.

Then a warrior dressed in black, carrying a sword and shield, went in and stood before the baby. And when he looked at the baby in the manger there was rage in his eyes.

"I hate you," he said. "You made a vile world. All my life I have seen the evil men do, and all my life I have fought it, which is more than you have ever done. But no matter how my times I hack down evil it rises again. And I have done such horrible things to stop evil that I am starting to feel like I have become evil myself. The human race is wicked and cruel. Just burn this world down and start over again. You can do better than this."

And the warrior looked down at the baby. And the baby smiled at the warrior. Then Jesus showed him the future.

The warrior saw Jesus as a man, trying to teach people to love one another. Jesus would grow up to be a man who did nothing but good, yet people would hate him. The warrior saw people plot against Jesus. Then he saw them arrest him and make false allegations against him. He saw Jesus beaten and tortured, but Jesus did not hit back. He saw Jesus nailed to the cross but he did not curse his murderers.

Jesus could have called on God to send an army of angels to destroy them all. Instead Jesus said, "Father, forgive them, for they don't understand what they are doing." Then he laid down his head and died. Jesus knew how evil people could be, but instead of destroying the world Jesus died to save it.

After this the warrior dropped his shield. He drew his sword and broke it over his knee. The warrior gave up his hate and he went into the world to fight evil by using the love of Jesus Christ. He loved people, no matter how wicked people may be.

And there are still many people in the world who are not wise. There are many who still do not understand. May all people of the world, no matter how wise they may be, come to that stable in that tiny town and see what the wonders this newborn king has to show you all.

www.ingramcontent.com/pod-product-compliance
Lightning Source LLC
Chambersburg PA
CBHW052140110526
44591CB00012B/1801